AF063329

Norman Handy

GOLD, IVORY AND SLAVES
Along the West Coast of Africa

novum pro

www.novum-publishing.co.uk

All rights of distribution, including via film, radio, and television, photomechanical reproduction, audio storage media, electronic data storage media, and the reprinting of portions of text, are reserved.

Printed in the European Union on environmentally friendly, chlorine- and acid-free paper.

© 2019 novum publishing

ISBN 978-3-99064-637-3
Editing: Hugo Chandler, BA
Cover photo:
Roberto Nencini | Dreamstime.com
Cover design, layout & typesetting: novum publishing

www.novum-publishing.co.uk

DEDICATION

For all the staff at Oasis Overland Ltd
who have arranged many of my trips
and who have looked after me so well,
to ensure that I always return safe and well.

CONTENTS

Chapter 1 – Moroccan Medinas 9
Chapter 2 – Agadir and Western Sahara 25
Chapter 3 – Mauritania 39
Chapter 4 – Saint Louis crossing into Senegal 51
Chapter 5 – The Gambia 59
Chapter 6 – Guinea-Bissau 71
Chapter 7 – Guinea Conakry 77
Chapter 8 – Sierra Leone 91
Chapter 9 – Guinea Conakry again 100
Chapter 10 – Côte d'Ivoire 105
Chapter 11 – Ghana 110
Chapter 12 – Togo 123
Chapter 13 – Benin 126
Chapter 14 – Nigeria 133
Chapter 15 – Cameroon 148
Chapter 16 – Gabon 164
Chapter 17 – Republic of the Congo 167
Chapter 18 – The Democratic Republic of the Congo 171
Chapter 19 – Angola 178
Chapter 20 – Namibia 189
Chapter 21 – The Skeleton Coast 202
Chapter 22 – Lüderitz and the Kolmanskop Ghost Town ... 215
Chapter 23 – South Africa 226
Other books by the same author 228
A message from the author 233

CHAPTER 1
MOROCCAN MEDINAS

Whilst en route to Africa, I took the opportunity to revisit Gibraltar. My first visit was at the height of a long hot summer some years before, as a day out, whilst staying at the family holiday home in Marbella. After the drive along the coast road to get there, I parked the car in Spain, and I walked across the border into Gibraltar.

Being such a small area, every bit of land is used, and crossing the border on foot is an experience. The main road crosses the runway. When a plane is about to land, the road is closed with a bit of string slung across the road. I had started walking across but I noticed that there was no one else coming towards me or following behind me. I thought it odd that some people in uniforms were waving at me, until I realised that I was alone in the centre of the runway and an aircraft was coming in to land, seemingly with its lights focused on me. It was an uneven match and I started running to get out of the way.

I found that the place was crowded, sticky, hot, and smelt of sewage. This was the result of an excess of pressure and untreated sewage that shot up out of a manhole cover and ran down the main road. I climbed up to the top of the rocks and the monkeys grabbed at cameras and bags, their sharp finger nails scratching exposed skin. There didn't seem to be much to do that I was interested in, so all in all, it was a bit of a waste of a day.

In recalling my experience of the place, many people were surprised as their experiences had been much more favourable. Therefore, I was quite surprised to find that after some researching of travel guides, that there is in fact quite a lot to see, and I had planned a couple of days to look around. Despite having a border with Spain and covering just 6.7 kilometres, it has been an enclave on the Spanish Mediterranean coast since it was captured by an Anglo Dutch force in 1704, during the War of the Spanish Succession, and ceded in perpetuity to the United Kingdom, as part of the Treaty of Utrecht signed in 1713; in part to ensure that Britain exited from the War of the Spanish Succession. It is an ideal naval base, as it controls the Strait of Gibraltar at the entrance to the Mediterranean, which is just thirteen kilometres wide at this point.

Technically it is a British Overseas Territory and there are thirty thousand who have voted repeatedly to reject unification with Spain. They are self-governing but Britain is responsible for foreign affairs and defence. The economy is based on tourism, financial services, gambling and maritime services.

I was hungry so I headed off to the city centre and I found a nice restaurant in the central square just by the bus station. I had a prawn tikka masala as I was unlikely to get a seafood Indian curry again for a while and I do like a tikka masala. I then walked along the lower coast road, passing the shipyards, the hundred ton gun, a sandy beach and I walked through three tunnels that the road took to get to Europa Point. There is a lighthouse and a mosque, several gun emplacements and a view across the straits to the coast of North Africa. It is not far away and can be seen on a good day but there was a haze, and it was an indistinct smudge on the horizon.

I walked back along the busy main road with a plan to get up to the top of The Rock. When I was last here, it was a long walk to the top but there is now a cable car. It rises to the summit at an elevation of four hundred and sixty-two metres, and the surrounding area is a nature reserve. Here is where the approximately two hundred and thirty Gibraltar apes live, but in reality, they are Barbary macaques, a type of tailless monkey, and these ones here are the only wild Barbary macaques in Europe; but be warned as they still snatch at bags and cameras and they will steal food, especially ice creams, from children.

I visited the Moorish fort and the Second World War tunnels, a mass of man-made caves hollowed out of the rock to be used as storage, barracks, defence, hospitals and passageways. They are on the north side of the rock and cannot be shelled from the sea by enemy boats. The pre-war population was evacuated to England, Morocco and the Caribbean for the duration of the war, whilst The Rock became a vital staging post for convoys to supply Malta and the Eighth Army in Egypt. There is also Gorham's Cave where excavations have shown extensive evidence of Neanderthal habitation on The Rock.

Then it was time to meet some of the others who would be travelling with me through West Africa. Some of the group I already knew, such as the drivers and the guides; the dual roles undertaken by Kim and Gareth with whom I had spent five months touring South America. They had taken a ferry from England to Santander and then they had driven south through Spain to meet us in Gibraltar. By tradition, all overlanding vehicles have a name and this one had been christened Nala.

We met at the airport in Gibraltar, but we were going to stay at a camp site some distance from Gibraltar on the Spanish mainland. There were some housekeeping jobs to complete. We would be camping and cooking for ourselves. We split ourselves into cook groups whose job it was to decide what to cook, buy the necessary supplies from a kitty, and then cook an evening meal and provide breakfast, plus lunch if we were having a lunch on the truck. Sometimes, we might be stopping in a town and either go off to a restaurant or buy our own choice of food from a supermarket. We had some gas in a canister, but it was reserved for emergencies as we would be unlikely to be able to refill it en route, as every country had different fittings. Therefore, we had a couple of lockers of wood. But cooking over a wood fire twice a day would soon use up our supply of wood, so whenever we stopped, we would scour the area for more fuel, but we needed to have enough wood to get us through the desert where there would be no opportunities to find more.

Not everyone had brought the right number of photos for their visas, the right currencies or inoculation certificates, especially yellow fever certificates, which would be required at several borders. There were also copies of credit cards to be taken, insurance details and a host of other things that needed to be sorted before we could proceed. It was our last chance to get everything in order, before we left Europe and crossed the narrow straits to land in Africa.

We boarded Nala and drove to the large Spanish port of Algeciras on the other side of the bay overlooking Gibraltar. Gareth drove the truck one way to join a queue of lorries, and the rest of us followed Kim towards the main terminal. This was a cavernous terminal building but being the low season, the few passengers that were here were lost in its vastness. We followed the corridors and the walkways and made our way to our ferry. It was a large ship, but it was empty. It had banks and banks of seats but only about ten percent were occupied. Certain areas were roped off and some of the shops on board were closed. It obviously becomes very busy during the high season to warrant such a large passenger terminal and ferries, but for us, we had a choice of places to sit and the opportunity to spread out.

We docked in Ceuta and filed off the boat. Although it is on the north African coast, it is still a part of Spain so there were no customs or passport controls at the port. I had often wondered how Spain came to have some enclaves on the Africa coast. The city was captured by John the First, king of Portugal in 1415 and it remained in Portuguese hands until there was a succession crisis in 1580 when Phillip II of Spain was crowned Phillip The First of Portugal. The Iberian Union continued until 1640, with the end of the Portuguese Restoration War, when Portugal regained its independence. Meanwhile, Ceuta had attracted a lot of colonists from Spain and they had sided with Spain during the conflict. It was only later under the terms of the Treaty of Lisbon in 1668 that Portugal acknowledged Ceuta's political reality and ceded the territory to Spain.

It covers an area of 18.5 kilometres^2, nearly three times the size of Gibraltar. Just as Spain periodically calls for Gibraltar to be returned to Spain, Morocco insists that Ceuta (and Melilla, another enclave on the north African coast covering an area of

12.3 kilometres^2 occupied by Spain since 1497), should be restored to Moroccan sovereignty but they refused, and the local populations prefer to be Spanish rather than being forced to be Moroccan citizens.

It was just a short drive along the coast road to get to the border. There were a few cars going into Morocco, but most of the traffic was queuing to get into Ceuta. The border crossing was relatively quick, and we drove on to Fnideq and we stopped to change our money. Finally, I felt as if I was starting my African odyssey to travel from the Mediterranean coast down the West Coast of Africa to the very southernmost point in South Africa.

We drove along the coast and turned inland to pass through Tetouan, a major town with a well renowned medina or old walled city centre. The city had plenty of green grass and trees, tall whitewashed buildings and was seemingly clean, tidy and well maintained. As we left the city and reached more rural areas there was more rubbish in the streets and plastic bags blowing across the fields as we climbed into the Rif Mountains.

We followed a river valley up into the hills. The fields gave way to steeply sloping hillsides and occasional tiny fields and mountainsides covered in olive trees. There was a new dam being built out of concrete and a saddle dam to one side. Some of the trees that would be flooded had been cut down but there was still plenty of work to do. Further up the valley was another already completed dam and over the pass was still a third older dam. I was surprised at the dams as I think of Morocco as an arid desert country but the winds coming off the Atlantic hit the mountains and drop a lot of rain.

We reached our campsite on the slopes above the town of Chefchaouen, bathed in the warm afternoon sun. It sits at an altitude of six hundred and seventy metres, but if a cloud came over or you walked into the shade of the trees, it was noticeably cooler.

It had been a cold night and our breath misted in the cold early morning air. We had time to explore the medieval walled city of Chefchaouen that has survived with little modernisation to spoil the city. It was founded in 1471 to resist the invasions of

Portuguese armies plundering the area. It is known for the various shades of blue in which many of the buildings are painted.

From our camp site high above the town, it was a downhill walk past several graves on the hillside and through one of the gates in the city wall. Inside was a maze of narrow steep streets. The town is one of the oldest unspoilt medieval Islamic cities that still exists virtually unaltered. It receives a lot of visitors in the high season and the authorities make a great effort to keep the place clean.

In the centre of the town is the kasbah or fortress which is open to the public. It has a central tower and a modest space enclosed by thick tall walls. The main square is under the shadow of the fortress and it is filled with market stalls selling handicrafts, clothes and tourist trinkets.Down the road from the square is the bus station and another square which is overlooked by three municipal buildings, and nearby is the central market where prices are low and there are all sorts of fresh produce on sale. I was part of the cook group with Sarah and Kenny. Sarah was travelling with her husband and they were entrepreneurs from Australia. They had sold their caravan park that they had developed for more than ten years and they were travelling around the world before returning home to build their dream home. Kenny was from the USA and in his twenties but he had had so many jobs working for different companies that I lost count; it was as if he was unable to hold down a job for long before moving on. But the common theme in all of them was that he was a truck driver.

We needed to go shopping but I didn't need an excuse to wander around a market and view the local produce with all the different colours and shapes of the fruit, vegetables and fish on offer, which I don't see in my local supermarket.

One of the challenges of camping and cooking is how to keep food fresh. We had cool boxes, but the challenge was to find ice to keep everything cool. We had decided that we were going to do a stir fry. We had bought some meat, but it needed to be kept cool. This is easier said than done, and I was tasked with finding ice whilst Sarah and Kenny carried the food back to camp. I asked around the market and eventually I found some, but after I had bought it, I had to get it back to camp before it melted. I walked to the nearest taxi rank and with the melting ice dripping water down my front and into my lap, I got a lift back to the camp.

It was a cold night and some people didn't sleep well as it was so cold, and they were up early. They had lit a fire to keep warm. As part of the cook group's duties, I had to get up early to set up the kitchen, boil water for tea and get everything ready for the others. Another early morning job was to light a fire, but Kenny and Luis, originally from Portugal who had just finished managing a hostel in Lithuania and he was between jobs, and both were awake due to the cold, so when I got up to start breakfast, they had already started a fire so that was one less job to do. And then after breakfast we still had to pack away our tents, fill the jerry cans with water and then wash up the pots and breakfast things before we would be ready to set off.

We had a drive through the Rif Mountains past peaks along valleys with rough mountain pasture. We left the mountains and crossed a rolling plateau with vast ploughed fields and only a few trees. We stopped at a small market town for the market, and for the next two cook groups to buy supplies before arriving in Fez.

Fez is a great place. It is Morocco's second largest city after Casablanca, with a population of more than a million. It has the University of Al Quaraouiyine which was founded in 859 AD and is the oldest continuously functioning university in the world. In 1170, it was the largest city in the world, with over two hundred thousand people living in the cramped quarters of the city. It was the capital of Morocco until 1912 and has an impressive palace for the king but it is not open to the public. There are seven gates to the palace, representing the days of the week and inside the high walls are gardens covering two hundred and eighty hectares. Fez was also the place where we were joined by Mike. He was an American and a former director of IT for a major bank. He was between jobs and taking a career break to explore the world before returning to the rough and tumble of business life.

I walked through the Mellah, the Jewish quarter and it was a Friday, so it was very quiet as just about every shop was shut. Then it was a five-minute drive up to a castle perched on the top of a steep hill, overlooking the city. From this vantage point and with the help of a map, I could pick out all the major attractions, the walls of the city with the old city inside, and the new city spread around the outside of the walls.

On the return journey we stopped at a pottery co-operative that made ceramics and mosaics. The process of making the mosaics was explained and demonstrated to us. The patterns are awesome and intricate, and it can take weeks to make some of the larger pieces.

We took Nala back into town to be dropped off for a walking tour of the medina with a local guide. We entered through one of the fourteen gates through the thick walls that encircle the medina. We were taken on an extensive tour of the narrow alleys and streets through the old city. There were numerous shops, workshops and residences. Donkeys and carts are used to move goods around and you never quite know what is around the corner. Many of the alleys are hemmed in by three storey walls, and in places the walls have become unstable and have been braced against one another with thick timber to provide support.

We passed through a market area with fruit and vegetable stalls in the streets. Around another corner was a metal working area where various metal sheets were beaten into bowls, plates and decorative items. The city also has the Chouara Tannery dating from the eleventh century, one of the oldest tanneries in the world and no visit to Fez can be complete without a visit to the tannery. We were given a sprig of mint as we went in to help ward off the offensive smells coming from the tanning process.

The skins are left for days in various pots, firstly in a water solution of crushed limestone and pigeon poo to remove the last shreds of meat and hair. The skins are moved to various other pots and finally to the dye pots, to be given whatever colour is required. Only natural dyes are used, including the most expensive, which is saffron for yellow. It is a colourful sight and luckily for us it wasn't a hot day but in the heat of summer, it must stink.

We passed several weavers and arrived at a carpet warehouse set up in a former merchant's house. There were some spectacular examples of woollen and silk carpets with fine knots and beautiful coloured patterns. All the carpets are handmade, and some take months to produce. They are consequently expensive and not an impulse buy. I like the type of work but with champagne tastes and beer money, the ones that I like most are the ones I can least afford and tend to be the most expensive.

Back at our campsite we had to do some paper work. We would be moving on to the capital, Rabat. We had various visa forms to complete for countries further down the coast, such as the Ivory Coast, Mali and Mauritania, which we would be obtaining while we stayed in the capital. Travel is easy but getting the necessary paperwork to cross borders is becoming an increasing challenge.

We stopped at Volubillis, a large ruined Roman city. It was already a settlement before the Romans arrived, but they developed it into a city. It sits on a confluence of two rivers, so it had an excellent water source and a good defensive position. The scenery around the city was a lot of the same rolling hills that we had been driving through all day, with fields and olive groves upon which the wealth of the city was based. It was abandoned in 808 AD when the king moved his imperial capital to Fez and the city shrank and eventually became deserted. It suffered badly from an earthquake in the mid-eighteenth century and the stones from the city were looted by builders who used the ruined city as a quarry, to construct the nearby city of Meknes.

After Meknes we took the motorway to the outskirts of Rabat, the present-day capital of Morocco, to find a bush camp. It was in a forest of cork oaks and most of the trees had had the bark peeled off the bottom section to be used for making wine corks, insulation and tiles and any of the other dozen uses possible for the bark. The campsite and the picnic area was a clearing in the forest, and there were posts put into the ground to control traffic, so that it didn't spread too far into the forest. However, there were intermittent gaps in the posts and a ranger directed us through the line of posts and up a track and over the brow of a hill, so that we were out of sight just as we had requested.

Being further away from the usual camping pitches, there was plenty of firewood so we didn't have to use any of our own. In fact, we filled up the last bits of space in the lockers with more wood. Wood is a precious commodity and we would conserve it as best we could, as there would be days when we could not re-supply as we crossed the desert further to the south. There were lots of pine trees and pine cones on the ground. These are excellent to get a fire going so Kim, Sarah and I got a large carrier bag and filled it with pine cones. The wood locker was already full, but the locker holding my baggage was only half full. It was meant for two people, but we didn't have a full complement of travellers, so I had a locker to myself, therefore there was some spare space, so the pine cones got stashed in my locker.

We packed away the bush camp and drove into the centre of the city. We crossed the river and drove up the bank on the far side and turned off the main road and parked outside the Ivory Coast Embassy. Then we went in one by one, to hand in our completed forms, have our photos and our finger prints taken. While we waited, we filled in visa forms for Mali and Guinea as we would also be getting these in Rabat.

It took all morning to process us, so after that, we had a truck lunch opposite the embassy and then we drove to the outskirts of Mohammedia on the coast for a bush camp on the beach.

I took a taxi into the centre of Mohammedia and bought a train ticket for the half hour ride into Casablanca. This is Morocco's largest city and it has a large port with a concentration of industrial plants. It is also famous for the third largest mosque in the world, the King Hassan II mosque, built right on the beach and half of the site juts out into the sea. It is a very large building and can house twenty-five thousand worshippers inside and eighty-five thousand in the square in front. Entrance is only allowed by a guided tour, and there are only four tours a day, so you must be on time, but the artistry and the craftsmanship is exquisite, and it is well worth making the effort to visit. It took six years to build at a cost of USD600 million. The city is also the setting for the Humphrey Bogart film, Casablanca, famous for that quote, and for Rick's café which exists, located between the mosque and the railway station.

It was an early morning start to get ourselves and breakfast ready for six thirty a.m. for a seven thirty a.m. departure to get back to Rabat to collect our Ivory Coast visas, passports and yellow fever inoculation certificates from the embassy. Then we drove around the corner and we then queued up for the next visa, at the Guinea embassy. However, they didn't need to see us in person, so Kim took all our passports and forms into the embassy and we had some spare time.

We parked in a large hypermarket car park on the outskirts of the city. Whenever we left the truck parked during the day, there were always two people assigned to stay on the truck to act as guards and we took it in turns to do the truck guarding whilst the rest of the group walked into the centre of Rabat to view the medina, the mosques and the museums. I had the first truck guard duty for the first two hours. This would give me some time to read the guide book and plan my day and I would also have the whole of the next day after collecting our passports from the Guinea embassy, to go sight-seeing.

We left in the late afternoon to go back to our old forest bush camp where we had stayed a couple of nights previously. We felt that we were going back to a well-known place, as we knew how to drive through the forest avoiding the lower branches and wooden posts, where there would be plenty of fire wood and where the thickest vegetation was, for privacy.

In the morning we had packed everything away even though we knew that we would be coming back to the same place that evening. We had a day to explore Rabat. However, disaster struck straight away. The truck became stuck in some soft sand and it wasn't going to get out easily. We all got off and tried pushing, as Gareth revved the engine and threw great clouds of sand into the air behind the truck into the faces of the pushers, but the truck didn't move.

It was time to get the sand mats out. We unlocked the long metal panels and dug some sand out of the area between the tyre and where the sand mats would be placed. There was a gentle gradient between the bottom of the tyre and firm ground. The sand mats were pushed in and we all stood back. Gareth gunned the engine and slipped the clutch and the truck was out of the soft sand. He didn't stop but kept on moving until the truck was on firm ground, near the main track of the fire break through the forest, and we then picked up and carried the sand mats back to the truck.

Then it was back to Rabat. Nala was left in the car park of a Manjane Centro Comercial, which is a large chain of supermarkets and I walked across the river to Sale Medina to explore the new town. I then caught a tram towards the old town and walked through the mellah and the medina, to the kasbah. There were some great views across the river and out to sea but there was little to see in the way of exquisite architecture or defensive structures. It was mainly functional.

I walked back through the medina and I came out by the gate to the south west. I took a wrong turn and I finished up in the far west of the city. I was next to the tram tracks and I worked out where I was and therefore where I needed to go, to get to the place where I was supposed to be. I caught the tram back from Place Russiye, but on a whim, rather than stopping at the Medina Kasbah, I stayed on until the next stop which was Chellah. Unfortunately, the tram stop that was named Chellah and the place that I wanted to visit that was also called Chellah were not in the same place. I walked back to the railway station from where I could remember the major streets and I started again.

I stopped off at the local liquor store. It was a nondescript entrance with no shop display, but it had every type of alcohol that you might want. Being a Muslim country, alcohol is not easy to find. Unlike in some countries it is not illegal, just frowned upon, so shops selling it like to remain low key. So, if you like a drink now and again and when you get the chance, you fill up with as much as you can carry. The shop was just a door and inside was a short passageway that opened out into a standard sized shop with shelves stacked with all sorts of wines, beers and spirits.

There was no rush and I spent some time in deciding my order. There was a counter, and you had to tell the staff what you wanted from the high stacked shelves behind them. It was very relaxed, and nothing was too much trouble. I asked to read the labels of several bottles. Most spirits at home have a standard strength of 40% but here there were a whole host of alternative strengths. Some were only 37% or 35%, while others were 43% or 45%, so comparisons had to be made, not only by price but also by alcoholic strength.

I finally bought a selection of local wines, putting the bottles in my rucksack out of sight, and then I made my way out past the royal palace to the Chellah that I wanted to visit. This area was abandoned in the thirteenth century in favour of the Sale Medina which was nearer to the sea, the harbour and was also a good defensive location. The Chellah area today has some exquisitely restored walls, but the inside was changed to gardens several decades ago. There are some structures to see but many of the previous city's buildings are now just ruins. The gardens were nice to see but there is little of any of the original buildings to view.

I walked back down the road that goes around the outside of the walled city back to the Majane Centro Comercial. I had not visited the King Hassan II mosque that morning, and although they are adjacent on the map, there was a cliff between the road and the site, so there was no access. I dropped off my rucksack and walked up the road to reach the walled city and then along to the mosque and the mausoleum.

We drove back the twenty or so kilometres to the campsite in the cork oak forest. We were there early and set up camp. I took a bottle of water that I had bought at Marjane and disappeared into the forest for a bush shower. I had to use my own water, as the drinking water on the truck is strictly for drinking and cooking and not for washing. If you want to wash, then you must provide your own water.

A job that had to be done when we bush camped was to find wood. We had wood, but as we went further south both water and wood would be difficult to find, so we had to use it sparingly and replenish our supplies whenever we could. The previous day's cook group were on wood duty to go and find as much as they could. Hence, they went off into the forest and came up against a first for the trip. Under one bit of wood they found a scorpion. It was a small sandy coloured specimen.

The emperor scorpion is black and can grow to twenty centimetres but luckily it is not dangerous. There are 1,500 types of scorpions and most have a sting but only fifty are lethal to humans. They use their sting and claws to hunt insects and they have an undeserved bad reputation. They look fearsome and ugly but are mostly harmless. Most stings are like a bee sting, but some people do have an allergic reaction. The smaller lighter coloured scorpions are often more dangerous. The one we had disturbed woke up and stretched its claws forward menacingly and walked away whilst we watched.

Gareth purposefully avoided the soft sand where we got stuck yesterday, only to find another soft spot. The back tyres sunk up to their rims. We got the spades out and started digging while the sand mats were unbolted from the sides of the truck to be placed under the tyres. Then Gareth revved the engines and drove off the soft sand. He didn't stop until he reached the solid ground of the fire break. Meanwhile, we carried the sand mats through the forest until we reached the truck and loaded them back on to their pegs. We were becoming old hands at digging the truck out of soft sand and using the sand mats.

We drove into Rabat and parked, near the Guinea embassy to retrieve our passports. Despite the 'getting bogged down in the sand incident,' we were still there early, but what we didn't know was that the lady who works at the visa counter didn't start work until ten thirty a.m. so we had another enforced 'chilling out' hour on top of the wait for the visa.

We got our passports and visas later that same morning and moved straight on to the Mali embassy, getting there before midday. The official said that we should have obtained the visas in our home country. Kim was clutching seventeen passports from nine different countries. The nearest embassy for the Australians and New Zealanders would have been Tokyo, but the official understood our position. He said that he would make a few phone calls to the capital in Bamako, and he suggested that we come back at two p.m.

Kim went back at two p.m. and all the passports had been stamped with visas during their lunch time. I dare say that they don't get many tourists and are only too happy to co-operate to encourage tourists. So, ten out of ten for Mali co-operation and speed.

As we drove away, several cars behind us hooted their horns. Someone hadn't closed the locker probably and we were dropping wood out of the locker on to the road. One of our group, Stefano, a student from Italy who had worked in IT in Germany had used the opportunity to set up his array of solar charging panels and had put them on the roof. We had set off and he had forgotten about them. As we bumped along the main road dropping wood, the solar panels had worked their way to the edge of the truck roof and had finally fallen off. We stopped and Stefano ran back to pick up his solar panels, and the rest of us walked along the road, picking up the lost wood. When Stefano got back on board the truck, there was a distinctive tyre mark right across the centre of his solar panels. Luckily, they are flexible and surprisingly robust and despite having had the weight of a car run over them, they still worked.

We had finished our chores for the day by obtaining our Mali visas and having our passports back in our hands by two p.m. The schedule is flexible for occasions just like this. Had we finished earlier we would have gone on to Marrakesh. Had we finished late in the afternoon, we would have returned to our bush camp in the cork oak forest despite the soft sand. However, it was just after two p.m. so we could break the journey to Marrakesh and return to the same campsite that we had stayed at earlier in Mohammedia for hot showers. When camping, some things such as good toilet facilities and hot showers are a rare luxury, so everyone was happy. We had the same pitches as before, and as we were early, we had the afternoon to do as we pleased.

CHAPTER 2
AGADIR AND WESTERN SAHARA

We took the motorway and headed for Marrakesh, stopping off in Settat for shopping. We also had a bonus when we arrived in Marrakesh. Our plan was to arrive in Senegal on a Thursday, but our hosts and minders suggested that we arrive on a Friday. There was various paperwork for the truck that needed to be officially stamped. If we were to arrive on a Thursday, we would have to drive straight to Dakar, the capital, to have the papers stamped the next day. By arriving on a Friday, the office would be shut for the weekend, so we could get some extra days and therefore take our time to see the national park, just over the border, rather than rush to have the paperwork stamped. Therefore, we had an unexpected extra day, so we would spend it in Marrakesh.

We now had three nights in Marrakesh. I had wanted to spend a night in a riad, which is a traditional Moroccan house or palace, with an interior garden or courtyard and because of their charm, many have been converted into hotels. But it was too late to book a night for the first night, and we would be leaving early on the last day and I would have to be up very early to get back to the campsite outside of town, and I was on cook group duty for the middle night. So, I missed my night in a riad.

Kim and Gareth had jobs to do either working on the truck or going into town to complete paper work. We needed truck guards for the day while some of the group headed into Marrakesh. There were two volunteers to truck guard for the whole day; Mikkel and Rowan. Mikkel was from Denmark. He was a former chef who had changed careers and was now a care worker. Rowan was a tall attractive pharmacist from New Zealand. Whilst they guarded the truck at the camp site, the rest of us hired a minibus to get into the centre of the city. It was en route that we saw several camels at the side of the road or tethered to palm trees. We had been in Morocco for a couple of weeks, but this was our first sighting of camels and we gawped out of the windows as our minibus raced by. We were dropped off near the centre of Marrakesh, outside one of the fifteen gates into the medina. We had gone in together, but we soon split up as we all had different plans.

The first place of interest for me was the mosque, followed by the central square, the Jemaa el-Fnaa. This square is alive with activity throughout the day with storytellers, acrobats, snake charmers, henna tattoo artists, musicians and loads of hawkers selling just about anything and everything. A nightly ritual sees hundreds of food stalls transform the square into one of Africa's largest street food areas with the aromatic smells of fresh local food cooking on charcoal braziers drifting across the square, to entice locals and tourists alike. There were several Africans dressed in traditional clothing, selling African art plus local Moroccans selling argan oil, figs, oranges, pomegranate juice or simply coffee from a thermos.

I walked through the bazaar just to see the sights, the colourful wares on offer, the different coloured fruits and vegetables and the arrays of leather goods and fabrics. Some areas specialised in jewellery. I walked right through the old city to the new city on the far side of the medina, where there were several blacksmiths working at their anvils in the heat of both the day and the heat given off from their forges.

I went back to the main square via another route. I didn't have a map, but I relied on my sense of direction. That was okay but there were several dead ends that required me to double back and try another route. I made my way around several palaces, gardens, mosques and around more stalls in the bazaar.

After a while walking around the city, it was time for lunch and I chose a restaurant at random and had a Salade Niçoise, freshly pressed orange juice and coffee. I had a little more time to explore before the minibus arrived, and so just nine of us returned to the campsite.

Several members of the group Mike, Luis, Dazzle and Noodles had decided to upgrade and stay in a hotel in the city. Therefore, we would not be seeing them for a few days. Dazzle was an independent building contractor from Australia, taking some time out. Noodles was a Canadian who had taken time off from her job, working for a wine, beer and spirit importing company who had rented out her apartment and was travelling the world.

I would have also upgraded, but I was a bit late trying to find a hotel, and I was on cook group duties, so I was a bit jealous. It was only that morning that Rowan had volunteered to swap with me, so that I could stay in the city. However, I was very specific about what I wanted, not just any riad in the old city, but one with a swimming pool, but all three choices were booked up. There were other rooms available, but I was very specific in my requirements, so I was on the minibus back at the camp site to join in the barbecue that evening.

The next day, Luis, Stefano and Kenny hired a taxi for the day, and went off to see the Atlas Mountains. Kim and Gareth had jobs to do to ensure that the truck was mechanically sound, and that all the paper work was up to date. Mat, Sarah and I did the truck guarding duties between us for the day. I had some emails to write and laundry to do so, other than that, I was going to have a lazy day in camp.

We left Marrakesh to drive to Essaouira on the coast. En route we stopped at the side of the road. There were several goats up in one of the trees. They climb up the trees to get to the fruits of the argan trees that grow profusely in the area.

A little further on, we stopped at an argan oil co-operative. There is a co-operative in nearly every village in this area. They are often women-run co-operatives that have been set up with encouragement from Princess Lalla Salma, the wife of King Mohammed VI of Morocco to help the women to obtain an income.

After the goats have eaten and digested the outer covering, the nuts pass through the digestive tract undamaged, but are stripped of their outer coating. They are then collected and brought to the co-operative. There was a demonstration of how the nuts are shelled by hand and then they are put through a pestle and mortar process by hand. The juices are extracted and refined and made into all sorts of products, such as cooking oil, skin products, cosmetics, medicines, soaps and a range of other products, all available to buy from the co-operative shop.

When we arrived in Essaouira, I headed straight for the harbour for a fish lunch. The harbour is set in a bay, protected by an island, so it is in an ideal location and Roman and Carthaginian remains found here indicate that it has been in use for millennia. Today it has a thriving fishing fleet. The fish are laid out on ice and you can choose your fish and it is gutted and cooked in front of you. It was early and all the café owners were imploring passers-by to come into their establishment. I purposefully walked past the pushier owners and I found a quieter café, set back from the main thoroughfare. I choose my selection of fish and I settled down.

After a leisurely lunch, I walked around the harbour, past the harbour defences, past the fishing boats bobbing up and down in the slight swell and I walked into the city. Essaouira is a corruption of its Arabic name meaning 'little rampart' although the walls seen today were only built in the 1760's, on orders from Mohammed III and the city was formerly called Mogador. I walked around the city walls as much as I could, only missing out a few sections that were either not open to the public or undergoing refurbishment.

Gareth then drove back up the Marrakesh road, looking for a bush camp in the scrub forest. We turned onto a forest track and went past one potentially suitable stop, but we didn't find another, so there was some delicate turning around and we parked diagonally across the track, to set up the kitchen, and then we set up the tents in a row on the track, as there was nowhere else that was flat and shrub free. We just hoped that no one came along and wanted to get past.

We were back in Essaouira for another brief visit. We had planned to stop at the Carrefour supermarket to stock up but it didn't open until ten a.m. so we parked outside the city walls and we had more time to explore.

Whilst walking about the city, I passed a bottle shop and since I was out of wine, I stopped and I bought a few bottles. I like wine with a meal, but it is hard to find in Morocco, and despite having their own wine industry, many shops don't stock alcohol. I made the most of this unexpected opportunity and I bought six bottles.

After lunch, we set off down the coast to Paradise Valley en route to Agadir. We drove through hills with a scattering of trees and a few fields and olive groves. The forecast for the next day was a 60% chance of rain. It was hard to believe as it was sunny and warm, and there were only a few small white clouds being blown up the coast. But the wind at that altitude was quite strong, and as we drove south the clouds became thicker and darker.

We turned off the main road at Aourir and headed up Paradise Valley. It was a very scenic drive up the valley and one of the best scenic routes in the country. However, the drawback was that the rainy season hadn't started yet and so there wasn't any water in the bottom of the valley; just a dried-up river bed, with a few puddles, which interestingly detracted from the alleged beauty and the waterfall was just a bare rock face.

Gareth drove up the valley, but the road became very narrow. The road follows the edge of the dried-up river bed with just a little freeboard. The edge of the road was weak and crumbled in places and then it turned a corner and suddenly it became steep and narrow. However much we might want to see the top of the gorge and the promised beautiful walk, the truck was not able to negotiate this part. Also had we arrived at the end and it rained, we might be stranded either with a washed-out road or impassable because of flooding.

Gareth reversed five hundred metres back down the road. Other traffic had to back up to let us through until there was a passing place, where the traffic in front and behind us could pass and then Gareth reversed again until there was enough space to turn around.

We drove back down the valley and stopped at a small roadside souvenir shop. The owner sold a mixture of locally made souvenirs, bits of rocks and fossils, largely ammonites that are plentiful in the local area and jars of honey from his own hives, which were scattered across the hillside behind his shop. Behind the shop was a flat area used for parking and it was suitable for a bush camp with some trees for both privacy and fuel. The owner was happy for us to camp there, and he watched bemused, as we set up the kitchen and later at dusk, put up the tents.

It rained during the night with raindrops beating on the canvas. It wasn't heavy rain but under canvas it always seems worse. Dawn arrived and there were still thick grey clouds. It wasn't raining where we were, but the hills on the far side of the valley were shrouded in cloud and it was raining there.

The sensible thing to do was to take the tents down early, to stop them from becoming wet as those rain clouds were coming our way. Some of us were ahead of the game and had already started packing their tents away. The Americans were the last ones to take their tents down. Mike had an excuse, as he was part of the cooking group getting breakfast ready. Kenny was running on Kenny time, and never did anything in a hurry, being in his own little world. Conall shared a tent with Luis, Luis was eating breakfast and Conall was a late riser and he always missed breakfast. I hadn't spoken much with Conall, but I knew that he was a chef from America, but he spent most of the day asleep on the truck, but he might stay up at night and be one of the last to go to bed.

Noah was a bit of a flarcher who shared a tent with Stefano. Stefano spoke English but I think that his comprehension suffers when several people are speaking fast and all at once, and he may have missed the importance of the instruction to take the tents down before it rained. Noah was a chemical engineer from Texas and had only joined us in Marrakesh and he looked ill at ease in the group. It is always tough to be the only new face, when you join an established group.

When it started to spit, we hurried to pack everything away and we needed to pack away the kitchen and breakfast things as a priority, before we could take the tents down. We usually dried the cutlery, crockery and pans by flapping them dry by hand, before putting them away, but in the rain, they were becoming wetter from the rain faster than we could flap them dry. So, despite them being wet, the kitchen got packed away first and wet, then those people who had not yet taken their tents down could go and sort them out, by which time they had been standing out in the rain and they had to be packed away wet.

The onset of rain meant that we left the bush camp half an hour before the scheduled time. We drove through Agadir to the Marjane Supermarket on the far side of the city. We had some time to look around Agadir, but no one wanted to go far in the rain. It was worse for the truck guards, as there had to be one person outside at the bottom of the steps, and he would get wet as it was still raining. I was the person whose turn coincided with the rain and I stood outside and I became wet and cold.

I was truck guarding, but I was also meant to be part of the cook group going shopping. Sarah, Kenny and I were meant to go cook group shopping together, but I was truck guarding, and Kenny didn't show up, so Sarah had to go shopping by herself. It came to the time to go, as previously agreed, but Kenny was nowhere to be seen. We waited for a short while but had to get moving so Gareth drove a short distance to the nearby petrol station to fill up, while we waited. Kenny eventually showed up late, having found a MacDonald's but he didn't apologise for being late, or for missing the cook group shop.

We drove south out of Agadir for more than an hour before the ribbon development along the main road gave way to desert scenery and returned to unchanging desert. There was a patch of thin forest to break up the monotony, before it returned to desert and it started to rain again.

We were due to visit the beach but, as it was raining, it was cool, and the visibility was poor. We were happy to stay on the truck and head on southwards. We stopped at a service station and some of us got off to stretch our legs for ten minutes. We were all back on board except for Kenny who was once again late without an apology, or a reason why, and he was beginning to get a reputation.

After another hour we reached some mountains and the road climbed up into the hills, with tight hairpin bends to gain elevation up some steep slopes. On one corner was a lorry that had toppled sideways on a steep camber and another lorry was picking up the spilt load. The load was bales of hay. The relief lorry was already full, with several layers of bales stacked above the sides of the lorry. There were still a lot of bales on the ground, so it seemed that the first lorry was overloaded, and that all the load was going to be reloaded onto the other lorry, as if they hadn't learnt a lesson.

The road crossed a plateau and the mountains moved back into the middle distance. We passed through Guilmime, a large busy town that used to make money from its weekly cattle market and from ransoming seamen shipwrecked on the coast. There were noticeably more policemen here, and there were several checkpoints, but we had only been stopped once.

South of Guilmime, there was a prickly pear plantation. A furrow had been ploughed in the desert and a single leaf had been planted at regular intervals along the widely spaced furrows. It was not a recent endeavour and some of the prickly pears had not survived and others looked to be desiccated. Once established, they grow like weeds, and are drought tolerant, but this new plantation seemed to be struggling to become established.

We turned off the road onto a track through the prickly pears. We found a dip that could conceal the truck and our bush camp from the road, but there was little privacy without walking a long way or waiting for dusk.

I had gone to bed early, but there were others who were awake till after midnight. They had checked the weather forecast and they saw that there was a fifty/fifty chance of rain. Therefore, they had taken the fly sheets out, and had put them over all the tents, just in case. They had done this without waking me, so, when I awoke and I wanted to get out, I was surprised that there was another zip and flap of canvas to negotiate. I wasn't panicking but I was a bit anxious for a moment.

It didn't rain during the night, but the extra cover meant that it was quite warm in the tent and with little air movement, there was a lot of condensation. We had to let the tents dry a bit while we had breakfast so that they weren't too damp before we put them away.

We drove on towards Tan Tan across the 'hammada' which is the local term for a stony desert. There were hills in the middle distance and occasional ridges to cross. There were no trees, only a lot of stones and patches of sand with a few scrubland plants, struggling to survive in the arid wasteland.

We crossed the Draa River which was the former border between Morocco that was a French sphere of influence and Spanish Western Sahara, an area that Spain had originally sought influence over, in the seventeenth century, to pursue the slave trade, but economic activity had shifted to fishing. This stretch of coast is opposite the Canary Islands, which Spain had ruled for centuries.

Spain occupied Western Sahara and established a colony there after the Conference of Berlin in 1885, which sought to establish rules of conduct and interaction for the European countries in their scramble for a share of Africa. In 1911, the Germans sought to exploit British and French tensions in their overseas policies, as international tensions rose in the lead up to the First World War. They sent warships to Agadir to support a rebellion against the French colonial rulers.

To counter German aggression, the other interested powers cut a deal amongst themselves. The French would recognise British spheres of interest in Cyprus and Egypt in return for France establishing a French Protectorate for Morocco. Meanwhile, the Spanish claims of control over Western Sahara were recognised and Germany received nothing.

Morocco gained independence from France in 1956 and two years later Spain gave Morocco a thin section of territory known as the Tayfaya strip which moved their borders more than two hundred and fifty kilometres southwards. The Spanish stayed until 1975 when they abandoned their territory in Western Sahara.

Morocco claimed the area, as did both Mauritania and the indigenous population who wanted independence and to establish the Sahrawi Arab Democratic Republic. Morocco undertook the Green March in November 1975 when three hundred and fifty thousand Moroccans marched south to colonise the area and to reinforce their claim, encouraged by the king. There was local resistance and the military moved in, creating a series of berms or sand walls to enclose an area which they then cleared of resistance, before moving on to the next area.

The area now has a tax-free status, and the government has invested heavily in infrastructure, building roads, bridges, hospitals, schools and social housing, plus numerous police and military bases. They are in full control of much of the territory except for a few thin strips of land beyond the berm bordering Mauritania, which the resistance fighters claim to control.

The indigenous people are fiercely independent, and a resistance movement grew that came to be known as the Polisario Front, with support from Algeria and Libya. Morocco countered this threat by moving in a hundred thousand troops. A ceasefire was finally negotiated, and a referendum was to be held, but neither side can agree who is eligible to vote. The basis of the disagreement is whether it is the people who live there now who should be allowed to vote or should it only be those who were born there before the Green March. The referendum has been postponed many times and it is unlikely to ever take place.

The road leaves Tan Tan and then follows the coast south on a rather uninteresting road along unchanging flat coastal scenery, only interspersed with the occasional estuary where a wadi has cut down through the cliffs to the beach. Here there were places where flamingos fed in the shallow sheltered waters and we stopped for a truck lunch on the cliffs overlooking a colony of flamingos feeding in the estuary below us. Nearby, is the Trou del Diablo, a large sinkhole where the sea had broken through at the base, to connect the bottom of the sinkhole to the open sea, through an arch of rock.

On a wide section of the beach, a little further along the coast, there were several salt pans and heaps of salt. There is almost constant wind in this area, which makes sitting on the beach unattractive, but it does mean that evaporation is encouraged for harvesting salt, an industry that has been located here for centuries. The wind is also used for modern day purposes as it is ideal for wind energy. The road passes row after row of wind turbines that generate electricity and send it to Laayoune, the capital of Western Sahara.

Finding a suitable bush camp was a challenge as there were few turn offs into the desert, and even if we made our own tracks, there were few ridges or dips to hide us from the road. We drove off the road and up a slight rise to find a plateau but at least it was some distance from the road. We could see some traffic, but we were several kilometres from the road and didn't expect anybody to notice us and come to investigate.

I was sharing a tent with Martin who was on cook group duties and he got up early. Martin was a software engineer from Sweden who was using part of his holiday entitlement for an extended holiday in West Africa. I was awake anyway, so I got up as well and helped the cook group to set up the kitchen, partly to keep warm but also partly because the sooner they set up, the sooner the fire would be lit, and the kettle would be hot. It wasn't all communal help as there was another self-centred interest in getting the kitchen set up. It was still dark, and it is difficult to have a shave with a head torch as the light is reflected into the mirror. Therefore, once the kitchen was set up, they would have the lights on, so that they could see what they were doing. I sat on a stool on the outer edge of the pool of light and used the overspill, to shave with the help of a small mirror.

After a long causeway across a flooded wadi we arrived in Laayoune, the regional capital. It has a population of two hundred thousand but it was only established as a settlement in 1940, so there is nothing historic to see. One of the few tourist things that are noteworthy is its oldest house which dates from just 1933. That shows how little there is to see here. It has a large military presence and it is also where the UN peace keeping forces and administration offices are located.

Just outside of the city to the south, the road crosses a conveyor belt that takes phosphates from the mine located inland at Bou Craa to the processing plant and export terminal at Port El Aaiún, to be shipped around the world. Phosphate is an essential fertiliser for farmers, and it is a major export revenue earner for the country. The country holds seventy-two percent of known mineral phosphate reserves and second is China with just six percent. Whilst some fertilisers can be manufactured, there is no known process to create phosphorous based fertilisers. Here is also the longest conveyor in the world at over ninety-eight kilometres. The wind blows some of the white phosphate dust off the conveyor to stain the otherwise brown desert in a long white strip that is visible from space.

We stopped for lunch on the beach and we went for a swim. The water was surprisingly warm, although I had been led to believe that it would be cold. There was also a large wreck nearby, but the currents were too strong to allow for a swim out to investigate it more closely. After lunch, it was back to the dull scenery along the coast road. We were lucky to find a hill near the main road with a track that went past it into the desert. We were not far from the road, but we were sheltered from it by the hill and other ridges around it, so it was ideal for a bush camp.

We scoured the hillsides around us for every piece of fire wood that we could find but it tended to be scrubland plants with dried twigs but no thick pieces, so it tended to burn brightly but quickly. We used that in preference to our own wood stock, but to get enough heat for embers to boil water for rice, we still had to use some of our own precious wood fuel.

That night there was a bright moon with clear skies, so clear that several of us saw shooting stars. But you had to be lucky to be looking in the right direction to see them as by the time that you said something and pointed it out, it had fallen to earth and was gone.

We stopped for a break on the main road opposite Daklia, which sits on a spit of land that runs parallel to the shore, and at its northern end, it is connected to the mainland. It was named the

Rio del Oro Peninsula by the Spanish, but there is no river and no gold, more of an aspiration than a name based on any reality.

In the distance were several giant sand dunes that rose more than fifty metres from the desert floor. They had the shape of a crescent moon, with a steep inner face and a gently sloping outer face. The predominant wind pushes grains of sand up the steep slope and drops them in the lee of the dune, to create a gentle slope on the leading edge.

We chose one of the larger dunes away from the road and parked within the horns of the crescent. We scrambled to the top, some making the difficult ascent straight up the steep face, whilst others walked along the gentle ridge that starts at one of the horns and curves up to the top.

There was a great vantage point from the top, but it was only barren stony desert floor with a few scrubland plants struggling to survive plus a few other individual dunes stretching away across the desert in all directions.

It wasn't a pleasant bush camp, as during the day, there was no privacy, and at night, it was difficult to dig a hole in the hard-stony ground. A stone free flat pitch for a tent was hard to find or it had to be made by removing stones and filling in gaps with sand or gravel. And then there was the relentless wind with sand stinging any exposed skin and covering everything with a fine layer of sand. The wind also blew sand onto your plate and covered your food with that extra crunch of sand against the enamel of your teeth.

Dinner was delayed although it was ready, as we had trouble getting the tents up. The ground was so hard that the pegs couldn't be driven home, even with hammers and some tents had to be repositioned. The wind made it difficult, as it was always plucking at any spare canvas and empty tent bags and anything else that would be blown across the desert if they were not held down. Old hands gathered rocks together in piles near their intended pitch, to be readily available and on hand to act as weights before trying to put their tent up.

But there were some plus points for this bush camp, as the dunes were nearby, and from the tops of the dunes, there were great views of the sunset and the moon rise. For those who were up early, there was also a great view of the moon setting and the morning sunrise.

Some of the group had changed their tent buddies and now Kenny and Noah, both snorers, had tents large enough for two people to themselves. Without another tent buddy to wake them up, they were the last ones to take their tents down; an easy job for two people, but difficult with a wind and doing it by yourself. Then just after sunrise, we bumped across the desert, back to the main road and we drove the forty kilometres to the border between Morocco and Mauritania.

CHAPTER 3
MAURITANIA

We arrived at the Moroccan side of the border shortly before ten a.m. and had our passports checked. Leaving a country is often straightforward but here it was different. We had our passports checked before we were allowed into the border area. Then we queued at another window to have our papers checked against their records of entries recorded when we arrived. We walked through another check point and waited for the truck. It had its papers checked for the insurance details, and the central computer records were consulted for any traffic violations. After the paper checks, it went through a giant scanner. Kim drove out of the truck scanner area, picked us up, and then we were through into no man's land.

There were a couple of UN cars in their white livery and 'UN' painted in big black letters on the sides. The tarmac finished and it was a bumpy, dusty drive across the sand of no man's land, for a few kilometres. It was a bizarre sight as there were tyres everywhere, hillocks of rubbish and abandoned vehicles, largely cars but also some trucks, mini-buses and vans. These were in all sorts of states from those that looked as if they had just been parked to others that had been stripped bare and were twisted rusted hulks. They are left here as they do not have the requisite papers such as insurance, proof of ownership, MOT certificates or equivalent, to be allowed to continue. Also, some were probably so mechanically or structurally unsound as not to be able to go any further.

We reached the Mauritanian border buildings. We joined the queue to have our passports checked and our details recorded on their system. We were photographed and each of us handed over fifty-five euros for the cost of the visa. Then each person's visa was printed and stuck into the passport. We were directed next door and we had to queue at the police station to have our details recorded again. We moved on to another queue to check that the details recorded on the police records screen were the same as those on the border immigration system, and that it matched the visa details held by the tourism ministry.

Only then did we get a stamp with a date over the top of the visa, to confirm that we could now enter the country. Customs officials came on board to do a quick search and they asked us whether we had any alcohol. Mauritania is a strictly Muslim country so the sale, and the consumption of alcohol is illegal; allegedly punishable by receiving forty lashes and a fine. Importing pork and pork products is also illegal and subject to large fines. We got back on board the truck and drove to the next checkpoint. Here we had our passports checked again, to see that we all had the right paper visa stuck into the passport and the right stamps, and only then were we allowed into Mauritania.

It seemed very bureaucratic, but it was best to have everything checked whilst we were still at the border so that we could go back and correct it before we left the border area. It was two thirty p.m. before we were through all the checks and driving down a tarmac road to Nouadhibou situated on a peninsular parallel to the coast.

The country derives its name from the ancient Berber kingdom of Mauretania, which existed from the third century BC to the seventh century AD and covered an area similar to the modern day area of Morocco and Algeria. About ninety percent of the country is arid Sahara Desert, so much of its 4.3 million population is concentrated in the south where there is more rainfall, and the capital Nouakchott has a third of the country's population.

The original Berbers were subjected to the spread of Islam and incursions by the Arabs. It was only in the late nineteenth and early twentieth centuries that the area was gradually absorbed into French West Africa. Mauritania became a protectorate in 1920 and later a French colony. It was administered from Saint Louis in present day Senegal, so that when Mauritania became independent in 1960, Nouakchott was chosen as the capital, as it was nearly central on the Atlantic coast even if it was just a small village at that time. There are still tensions and conflict between different tribes within the country, which adds to problems of poverty, drought, desertification and human rights issues. It is quite incredible to think that slavery was only abolished here in 1980 and it is rumoured that it continues in some rural areas.

We had anticipated that the border crossing would take a long time, so we only planned to drive less than fifty kilometres to Nouadhibou. This is a new city situated on the eastern side of a peninsula. The whole peninsula was part of Spanish Western Sahara but the west side was occupied by Morocco and the eastern side was occupied by Mauritania when the Spanish withdrew in 1975. Mauritania gave up its claim to the rest of Western Sahara, but it kept this small area of territory and the few houses that were there have grown into the city seen today.

The Banc d'Arguin National Park which is across the bay from the peninsula is a draw for bird watchers and an opportunity to see seals. This area looks over the Baia de Levrier and Nouadhibou, which is also a port and the terminus for the railway. For greasers, this railway is a great opportunity to see some of the longest trains in the world. The line runs for six hundred and fifty-two kilometres inland to the ore mines at Zouerat the main town, whose existence is due to the iron ore mining industry. These trains can be over two and a half kilometres long and have over two hundred wagons, each carrying eighty-four tons of ore. At the end of the ore train is a single passenger carriage, making it the longest mixed passenger train in the world. The train to Zouerat takes sixteen hours with empty wagons, but the train coming from the mines takes twenty hours to reach Nouadhibou. Other than trains and birds, there is little of interest to the tourist in the city itself, but it seems very different from Morocco, with its Arab, Berber and Saharawi influences.

As part of security for the group in this country, we could only go somewhere in groups of at least three. The cook group went shopping and I tagged along for the walk along with Gareth. The main shopping area has a lot of local shops and food markets, all functional and other than the shops, there was nothing of note or of historical interest.

There was no internet at the campsite, but the owner directed me around the corner to an internet café. Mike, Kenny and I walked around the corner and found the place. It was a bare room with computers around the walls with three customers and one member of staff, who was playing a game with three of his friends. It was cheap at the equivalent of a euro for an hour, but the speeds were slow and insufficient to download photos, films or to run any social media, but it could be used for emails.

We had also received some news which was both good and bad. The Nigerian embassy in Bamako in Mali was now no longer issuing visas to people who were not resident in Mali. This was a bit of a blow, as I wanted to see Mali and we had to go there to obtain our Nigerian visas. But a new alternative was now available which was to obtain our Nigerian visas in The Gambia which wasn't on our original schedule and this meant more border crossings and visas for the citizens of Portugal and the United States. We would be able to visit The Gambian embassy in Nouakchott whilst we were there, so that was one of the hurdles resolved, but we would not be visiting Mali.

We had breakfast at the campsite in Nouadhibou. I gave Dazzle a hand in filling jerry cans. There were a dozen twenty-five litre jerry cans of water to fill, add purification powder to and load onto the truck. We had come across the desert and we had used a lot of water which needed to be replaced. However, it was a low pressure tap, it took forty minutes to fill all the jerry cans and we were late for breakfast.

There would be more check points on the road up the peninsula, around the top of the bay and down the road to Nouakchott. We had a sweepstake to see who would correctly guess the number of road blocks. I was one of the early guessers and I chose twelve. People chose numbers between four and twenty-four. Luis chose four and Rowan chose twenty-four and as it turned out, I had chosen the mid-point of the range of numbers.

I hadn't read the weather forecast, but it was windy and there was a lot of fine sand in the air. It wasn't a full-on sandstorm and although the dust was fine, it didn't sting exposed skin. Instead, it just clogged in your hair and everyone's clothes turned a uniform sandy colour, with a gritty feel. It seeped in everywhere through the smallest of gaps and soon all surfaces were covered with a film of fine dust.

The scenery was unchanging; flat sandy desert with no hills and no trees to break the monotony. There were a few scrubland plants and in places, there was only sand. This is what many people think a desert looks like and we were driving through it all day with little change of scenery. It was bright, hot, dusty and windy without any let up all day. As we left the border area, the number of check points decreased and it was Jacci who won the sweepstake, having chosen ten. She was one of the few fellow English travellers in the group. By coincidence she lived not far away from me in Sussex. She worked for the council and she had taken an extended unpaid holiday so that she could join the group going through the whole of Africa.

Late in the afternoon the road changed into a three-lane highway, lined with solar powered lamp posts. It was far more than required for the light traffic on the roads, but this was the outskirts of Nouakchott, and they were obviously planning for a big increase in the population. There was construction being undertaken everywhere, as if the city was expanding rapidly.

We stopped at The Gambian embassy, as some of the group needed to obtain a visa whilst it was free entry for the rest of the group. We had missed closing time by just minutes, but they said that they would be happy to see us in the morning. We drove on to our campsite at Menata Auberge.

We were staying at a nice backpackers place with character, not far from the city centre. There were upgrades available and as usual, some of the group shunned the camping option and opted for an upgrade. There was an unusual upgrade that Kenny, Conall and Stefano took, which was to sleep in a round tent on the flat roof. With a little imagination, you could pretend that it was a bedouin tent and it was decorated inside with authentic artefacts and wall hangings, but from the outside it was a large round canvas tent on a concrete flat roof. But there were beds inside and given that it was high up on the roof, it caught any breeze, so it was probably the better option than a tent in the sheltered and the walled courtyard.

For the Portuguese, the Canadians and the Americans, it was a taxi ride to the Gambian embassy early in the morning and a long wait, whilst forms were filled in and checked. Then the process stopped for a lunch break and continued in the afternoon, while all the visas were issued. They had arrived at eight a.m. and it was after four p.m. that they were able to leave the embassy, but luckily with their visas in their passports.

For the rest of us it was a leisurely breakfast around the camp fire. The fire was lit, and we had held back, so that those who were going to the embassy could have breakfast first before they left. Then we started to cook our own eggs however we liked them cooked. There was an informal queue to cook eggs in the frying pan and to toast bread on the open fire.

We were standing around the fire, waiting our turn with eggs and bread in our hands. Someone would scoop their eggs out and the next person would position the pan, add oil if necessary and add their eggs. The frying pan had been returned to the fire but Mikkel upset several people. He came over to the fire and without checking or even noticing that people were queueing, he lent through the ring of people around the fire and cracked his two eggs into the pan. It was pointed out to him that there was a queue, but he just laughed, and he said that the frying pan was empty, and he had used it. Not even an apology.

Personally, I don't like my eggs cooked in a pan that is on a slope as the eggs run before, they turn white, so they become quite large. I like them underdone, on a low heat, the yolk still runny and in the deep crease of the pan to keep them together.

Mikkel likes his thin, spread all over the pan and turned over, and cooked to a crisp over a hot fire, which also leaves little bits in the pan which are hard by the time the next person uses the pan, unless they are all removed. I prefer to be either first and out of the way within ninety seconds or last, so I am not in anybody's way.

I had to find an internet café in order to download my bank details. This was one of the documents that would be required by the Nigerian authorities to support my visa request. It was to be used as evidence that I had enough money to support myself whilst I was in Nigeria and to be able to get out of the country. The internet was slow, the keyboard unfamiliar and in order to print, it wasn't a simple single click on the print icon but there were several hoops to negotiate through to find the page to print. A normally simple thirty second process at home took an hour where we were.

After grappling with unfamiliar keyboards and visa requirements, it was time for some sightseeing. The grand mosque was nearby, and I went to have a look at it. It was closed between prayer times, so I was not able to see the inside. It is a large but modern affair. The city was only chosen to be the capital in 1958 and then it was just a small village but with a deep water harbour and the capital was designed to house only an extra fifteen thousand officials.

It was a conscious decision to locate here to avoid existing bigger towns and cities and to avoid building a capital in either an Arab, Moor or Black African dominated area. It has since expanded with an influx from rural areas, due to a decrease in rainfall, an increase in desertification and a movement of population towards the city, in search of jobs. It is now home to more than a million, a third of the country's total population. It is such a new city that there is nothing of historic value to see. But one claim that I can make is that I have visited all the places with which the city is twinned, namely Madrid in Spain, Lanzhou in China and Amman in Jordan.

One of the few but popular sights to see according to the guide book is the fish market, which is set up on the beach where the boats land their catch, some five kilometres from the centre of town. A group of us walked there in the fierce midday sun. You could smell the place before you reached it. There were a lot of boats pulled up out of the water above the high tide mark and seemingly abandoned. There were more boats on the beach and yet more boats bobbing up and down at their moorings, just off shore. The boats were brightly coloured in primary colours.

All sorts of fish are landed here, straight from the sea onto the beach to be unloaded into boxes and wheeled up to the central selling area, a grandiose name for a patch of concrete with an ice plant next door. It was a hive of activity with carters pushing or dragging carts from the beach to the market. Sellers had their fish spread out on sheets or in baskets in front of them, to sell on to middlemen or to customers.

There were lots of people milling about, bag sellers, ice sellers, carts moving back and forth and all the colour and bustle of a busy market. It was a colourful sight, but the smell was strong, the temperature high. There was no shade and people were superstitious and they didn't want their photos taken, so I was glad to call it a day and find a taxi back to the hostel.

We were only moving on at midday, so we had a morning to ourselves except for those of us with essential things to do. Those who had been to the Gambia embassy the day before to get their visas now had to find an internet café to print their bank statements to produce alongside their visas at the border to prove that they had the funds to transit through the country, so that little job would take a chunk of their morning.

The cook group was Sarah, Kenny and me again, so we needed to go shopping. Sarah and I waited for Kenny, but he never showed, so we went off shopping and we blew the budget. We bought much more than was necessary, plus a water melon which is a thirsty crop and therefore expensive. All the other fruit and vegetables seemed to be quite cheap, but water melons seemed to be disproportionately expensive. We even asked the shop to cut it in half to reduce the cost, plus we put a few things back, but we were still over budget and we still had to buy bread and some beans for a bean salad. Any over expenditure had to be funded from our own pockets, so Sarah and I ended up digging deep into our own pockets to fund the difference.

We had packed away our purchases and we were ready for another excursion into the centre of the city. Martin was still in camp, so he and I went for a wander into the market to find a pharmacy. We hadn't gone far before we found some of the rest of the group having coffee at a café, so we joined them. Then it was a wander off to the main market, as both Martin and Mike wanted to buy headscarves to wrap around their heads, in the local fashion, to keep the dust out of their hair and faces and if it became bad, it could also cover their eyes.

After an evening meal around the camp fire and an early morning start to leave Nouakchott, we were driving through desert again. Desert is such a general term but covers a lot of different scenery types. There were more shrubs and occasionally, stunted trees. We passed through different areas, sometimes with shrubs, sometimes with a sprinkling of trees, and sometimes with nothing but sand and low undulating dunes.

En route southwards, we stopped for a break and as it happened there were a few trees. There were also several dead trees and branches which meant firewood, so these were dragged back to the truck. We used axes and saws to chop the wood up to fit into the wood lockers. It was hard work, as the wood grows slowly, and it has very close tree rings and can be as hard as iron or ebony.

Gareth came up trumps, and got the power saw out from the tool locker. It isn't used very often, so it is often buried at the bottom of a locker, so it rarely comes out. There was so much hard wood, and it was so difficult to saw through by hand, that it was worth the effort to get the chain saw out from the depths of the locker.

It made short work of the trees, cutting them into either long lengths to be stored under the truck with some spare sand mats, for chopping up later, or into short manageable lengths. These shorter lengths were loaded into the wood lockers, including a few that were spirited away into the bottom of my locker, to join the pine cones that still took up half of the locker that I was using.

We continued and there were an increasing number of villages and houses along this stretch of road. There were mosques, community halls and so many buildings with the same design, that it must have been a major government sponsored project to provide buildings for the local population.

We turned off the main road that would have led us to a major and very busy border crossing, plus a ferry to get across the river, in favour of a route through yet more desert to a quieter border crossing, and the opportunity to traverse part of the Diawling National Reserve, which was established in 1991 amid controversy, as it is adjacent to the Djoudj National Bird Park in Senegal, which was established in 1971. The locals in the Diawling area feared a similar restriction on fishing and hunting that had accompanied the creation of the Djoudj area.

The area is significant as it is a major flood plain area hosting both fresh water and saline wetland areas. It is a major feeding and roosting ground for many species of birds, and home to many patas monkeys, warthogs, wildcats, golden wolves and wild donkeys. It is also a malaria swampland and harbours bilharzia and invasive species.

Some of the larger mammals have disappeared due to drought, hunting and the construction of a dam. The last West African lion was last seen in 1970. The last red fronted gazelle was seen in 1991. Manatees, crocodiles and hippopotamuses, which used to be seen here have since also disappeared. But this last animal caused some discussion, the correct plural for hippopotamus is hippopotami, like the plural of octopus is octopi, but as the origin of the word is Greek it should be octopodes. But nothing is straightforward as the plural for syllabus should be syllabi but it is syllabuses. The actual plural depends on the origin of the word, but as English is a living language and includes lots of foreign words borrowed from other languages, I have opted to write this plural as hippopotamuses rather than the pedantic but correct version. And with usage over time, the incorrect – 'muses' ending will become the 'correct' plural.

The sign boards at the start of the park listed some of the more common animals that we were likely to see. It was getting towards dusk and this is the best time to see wildlife in their natural habitat. We saw our first warthogs, first it was just one, and then a family group of a mother, a father and a juvenile. Soon we were seeing dozens of them along the sides of the road. They aren't particularly attractive, but they do have their charms, and you never forget the time that you see your first warthog in the wild.

We had been talking about seeing the Big Five, being the five most difficult large game animals to hunt on foot. These are lion, leopard, rhinoceros, elephant and Cape buffalo. This original grouping was so successful with tourists, that other groups of five were created. Another group was the Little Game Five coined by nature conservationists to highlight smaller species, and as a bit of fun, used animals with a similar name but the opposite in size terms to the large game animals. These are the elephant shrew, the buffalo weaver bird, the leopard tortoise, the ant lion and the rhino beetle. Various commentators have since expanded the range, with some overlap to the carnivorous five, the ugly five and so on.

We passed an iguana that scurried away from the road as we passed. There were more warthogs as we drove along the edge of the beach, with its lagoons, islands and patches of vegetation growing out of the water. Birds flew up in great flocks as we passed, to obscure the setting sun. The wetland area provides a habitat for more than four hundred different types of birds. I saw a cuckoo with its distinctive tail, as it flew over the bulrushes. There were warblers singing in the reeds, and flocks of pelicans and flamingos' feeding in the shallow waters.

We came to yet another check point at a junction where the road that we had been travelling on joined a wider road, and we were now just fifteen kilometres from the border. We still hadn't found a good place to bush camp, but this checkpoint looked good and the guards were happy for us to camp there – but it came at a price. It had a lot of still lagoons. It was a mosquito infested area and together with sand flies and a host of other biting insects, it was picturesque but a hell for man. The only sweetener that the guards wanted, to let us camp nearby was insect repellent. A few ouguiya (the local Mauritanian currency) or food wasn't enough, (and we had a policy against bribes), the sweetener to let us camp was a high DEET percentage insect repellent.

The guards were delighted with their new albeit half empty pump action bottle of insect repellent, and they retreated to their campsite at the side of the gravel road that doubled as a security checkpoint, on the road to a remote border post.

We retreated to a flat area next to the road that would be our bush camp. We checked with the guards that we were able to light a fire and to cook a meal despite the large signs saying no matches and no cigarettes and to be aware of fires. We had our evening meal and as I was part of the cook group, I was cooking so I didn't have a chance to explore, but some of the others came back with sightings of yet more warthogs, crocodiles, other animals and a host of birds.

CHAPTER 4
SAINT LOUIS CROSSING INTO SENEGAL

It was a short drive to the border and our aim was to be one of the first in the queue to get through, to get into Senegal and to beat the crowds that come later and slow down border crossing checks. Then we planned to continue toSt Louis and on to our next campsite near the city.

We were at the border early, but we weren't the first. However, it was relatively easy to sign out of Mauritania and to cross the dam over the Senegal River and arrive at the Senegal border control. This was a visa-free border, with no money to pay, but it still took some time to have our fingerprints taken, pictures taken and details revealed of where we were going to be for the next few days.

It was all over in less than two and a half hours, which we would learn later was a quick border crossing in African terms, and shorter than the half-a-day to get into Mauritania. It was a short drive to an area near the centre of Saint Louis, which was the first French settlement in West Africa.

Saint Louis was the oldest town founded by the French colonists in Africa when it was captured from the Dutch, in 1659. The French had tried to capture Essaouira in Morocco to establish a colony in 1629 during a raid on Salé next to Rabat but had given up and returned to the main force which was repulsed. The oldest French colony had been established more than a hundred years before, in 1534, by Jacques Cartier on the Gaspé Peninsula, on the south shore of the Saint Lawrence River in Quebec in Canada.

It was from Saint Louis that expeditions spread out to conquer the interior, and French traders exported leather, beeswax, ambergris and gum arabic, the hardened sap of various species of acacia tree. It was also a major slave trading centre, and there is a memorial art installation on the port front on the island, to remind visitors to remember the tens of thousands of slaves who were taken from here to the Americas.

It was the capital of Senegal from 1693 onwards. There was a period starting in 1758 during the Seven Years' War when the area was captured by the British, who held it until French forces recaptured the city in 1779. In 1895, it became the capital of French West Africa until 1902, when the capitals of both French West Africa and Senegal were moved to Dakar, two hundred and fifty kilometres down the coast and approximately in the middle of Senegal's Atlantic seaboard.

The port of Saint Louis is more than twenty-five kilometres up the estuary and the river brings down a lot of silt, which forms numerous bars in the port approaches which shift over time. Larger steamships found the port at Saint Louis difficult to navigate, and preferred the port at Dakar, with its easier approaches and greater space. In 1885 the railway linking Saint Louis to Dakar was completed, and it took trade away from the port, so Saint Louis was declining while Dakar was expanding.

Under the terms of the Treaty of Paris in 1814, the European powers agreed that Mauritania would be a sphere of French influence, although actual control for the rest of the century was never very strong, and nobody asked the Mauritanians about it. In 1903, Xavier Coppolani, a French Algerian born to Corsican parents and a colonial military leader, persuaded several emirs in southern Mauritania to accept French rule in exchange for protection against other tribes. French rule moved northwards, but some of the more northern tribes weren't included in French West Africa for another three decades. When the new territories were upgraded into a French protectorate in 1920, it was ruled from Saint Louis in neighbouring Senegal until its independence in 1960.

The city of Saint Louis is located at the mouth of the Senegal River and is surrounded by the sea on one side and marshes that flood in the rainy season, on the landward side. It is an interesting place to visit and was added to the list of World heritage sites in 2000, due to its influence on developing education, culture, architecture and services over a large part of West Africa. It is also an outstanding example of a colonial city, helped in part by the transfer of the capital to Dakar, and thus, it's old centre and its architecture was not subject to extensive redevelopment.

The city has a very different feel to the Arab and the Berber influenced cities, and countries we had just come through. There were black faces everywhere, and we stood out as the only Europeans around and were unmissable in our large yellow truck which we parked near the market.I was on truck guard duty for the first hour and I watched the hustle and bustle of a colourful African market. Once my hour of duty was up and I was relieved, I had some time to cross the bridge over the Senegal River to see the old town on the island in the river. The island is two kilometres long, and not more than four hundred metres wide, but it is protected from the sea by a spit of land which forms the other river bank of the estuary. It was here that the first French settlers built their port facilities, warehouses and homes.

I walked around the area to gaze at the colonial architecture, but also to find a bank or a bureau de change to exchange some money. All I found was a restaurant on the river front overlooking the bridge, to sample a local fish dish, so I had lunch instead of changing any money. That was not a problem as I had brought a small amount of money for every country that I was due to travel through, just in case we crossed a border on a weekend or we were in a remote area, and there were no banks or money changers available.

I had wanted to visit the Saint-Louis Research Centre and the Documentation Museum of Senegal which, according to the guide book offers interesting panoramas of Senegal's history and ethnic movements (meaning politically correct terminology for slave trade) over the years, exhibitions of traditional clothes and musical instruments but I didn't have enough time then, but there would be another opportunity.

The city was a centre for sugar production but there was little evidence of this in the city centre. On the far side of the island is the local fishing port. It was crowded with boats decorated with patterns in mainly bold primary colours. The fish market was equally busy with fisherman selling their catches. Different tribes by tradition do different work. Fishing is dominated by Wolofs and Lebous whereas farming is dominated by the Fulas. The merchants, traders and shopkeepers are mainly Maures from neighbouring Mauritania.

Nowhere in the city is far from the sea, and nowhere is very high above the high tide mark. In June 2008, Alioune Badiane of the United Nations Habitat Agency described Saint Louis as the city most threatened by rising sea levels in Africa due to climate changes. And despite the assertion of imminent doom, not much has happened since.

We regrouped at the truck at about mid-afternoon, for the drive to our campsite at Zebrabar on the outskirts of the city. It was on the coast with its own beach, flat pitches for the tents, plenty of shade and soft sand everywhere, that made putting tent pegs in easy and there were no other guests. Plus, it had a bar. After weeks of having difficulty finding beer and then several days without any alcohol as it was illegal in Mauritania, as soon as the truck stopped at our allotted site several of the group headed for the bar. The celebrating was interrupted by dinner, and after dinner many of the group went back to the bar. I had had enough celebrating, rediscovering alcohol in its various forms and went to bed shortly after sunset. I woke up at one a.m. and there were still people talking loudly, slurring their words and continuing to party at the bar, which was doing a roaring trade.

Some of us were up early, and others would not be seen until after lunchtime, swearing that they would not drink ever again. It was said with good intentions and was probably true until it was time for aperitifs before dinner that evening.

It was a day to relax, go for a swim, walk along the breach, take a taxi into town or borrow one of the camp site kayaks or canoes and go for a paddle. There were tours available to be booked at the bar, such as taking a pirogue trip, going on a bird watching trip, a trip to the island nature reserve of Langue de Barbarie just off shore, or being taken to one of the best fishing spots along the coast. There was a lot to do and time to do it in, but I just had a leisurely morning. I would visit the museum another day. For lunch, I chose a typical Senegalese fish dish from the menu at the bar. I am always easily persuaded by any description on a menu that describes a dish as a local speciality, as I am always happy to try local delicacies.

After lunch, Martin and I booked two kayaks and launched ourselves off the beach. The sea here is calm as it is sheltered by the peninsula and there are several uninhabited islands that hug the coast which are nature reserves.

We paddled across the short stretch of sea water to an island and beached our kayaks. The islands are low lying sand bars, with a few trees and only a collection of shrubs. We paddled on to the next island but there was no more to see there than the previous island. It was mostly salt tolerant shrubs growing in sand and no fauna to see.

The cook group of Mikkel, Noah and Luis cooked dinner and then contrary to the previous night, most people went to bed early, except for a few who hung around the bar until nine p.m. and then they too went to bed. It wasn't an early start, as breakfast was served at seven thirty a.m. and therefore we only had to be ready to leave at eight thirty a.m. but it had been a long night the night before.

We left Saint Louis and drove south, to find a bush camp near the border with The Gambia. The scenery was noticeably different. The Sahara had given way to the Sahel, a vast area of savannah. There is a little more rain and ground water and there are more trees. Under the trees there was more undergrowth of briars, thorns, grasses and shade.

Then we had another couple of firsts for the trip. We saw our first Baobab trees. Just two of the nine species that are found in mainland Africa. They are distinctive as they store water in their trunks, so the trunk seems disproportionately thick, compared to their canopy. The heights vary between five metres and thirty metres with diameters of up to eleven metres, although the largest specimen was recorded in South Africa with a diameter of sixteen metres.

We also saw our first African huts called rondavels. These were small circular buildings with a conical thatched roof that finished in a point. The walls were a mixture of reed, mud on wattle or apparently quite solid made, of brick but it might have been whitewashed mud. It was hard to tell at a distance. Some were in a compound by themselves and others were in a group with a single wall surrounding several huts. There were some places that had upgraded their mud walls to breeze block and corrugated iron and some of the original thatched huts looked to be in disrepair and were used for storage.

It was a long drive throughout the afternoon. Some people read a book or looked out of the window. Others slept occasionally as we all do from time to time. Conall was something different. He was a bit of a night owl and would happily stay up talking and drinking until long after most people had gone to bed. He also didn't eat breakfast, so he would often appear as we were finishing breakfast to take down his tent, and then he would get on the truck and sleep for the rest of the morning.

Noah was also different. He said that he had travelled widely and had claimed to have seen many sights in different countries and that his travel aim was to visit as many different countries as possible. On this particular trip he spent eight to ten hours a day playing a game on his phone. He would occasionally look up if someone made a loud comment on a particular piece of scenery, but for the most part, he was glued to his phone. But it would be dull if we were all the same and it takes all sorts. Personally, I enjoy overlanding as I see so much more of the country and stare out of the window, but who am I to judge over people's idea of a holiday?

It was getting late in the day and we started to look for a bush camp just as we came to Touba, a major city and the second most populated city in the country. This is the holy city of

Mouridism and the burial place of its founder, Sheikh Ahmadou Bamba Mbacke. He had a vision whilst sitting under a tree and consequently founded the city here in 1887. He died in 1927 and was buried here. A large mosque was built next to his burial place which was completed in 1963. Touba in Arabic means felicity or bliss and is the sweet bliss of eternal life in the hereafter. In Islamic tradition it is the name of the tree of paradise.

It took us more than half an hour to get through the centre and back to the suburbs on the far side. We drove on, and eventually found a place away from the road. Although the scattering of trees was not enough to obscure us completely from the road or hide the lights of the trucks at night, nor did it dampen any of the road noise.

The ground was soft sand, and the truck got stuck a couple of times. There were many dead and dried plants growing under the trees, including some with wicked thorns and other plants with burrs, and multiple short but sharp spines. Our legs, shoes and clothes were soon covered in burrs and the thorns were unpleasant and painful.

We used spades, trowels and machetes to clear the worst of the undergrowth for a kitchen area and for our preferred pitch for our tents. The cook group got on with the cooking and the rest of us gave a hand to their tent buddies, to get their tents up before it became too dark.

The dried vegetation burnt fast, and gave a bright light, as the flames consumed the dried stalks, but it produced just a flash of light and heat, and then disappeared into ash. It was no good for cooking and our supplies of wood were becoming low so we would need to be parsimonious with our fuel burning and look out for more on our way to the border the next morning. As for camp site scores, the burrs and the thorns made this a one or two out of ten.

We were within earshot of a village and the muezzin woke us up at five thirty a.m. and after a struggle with the sand mats to get the truck over the soft sand, we were soon back on the hard tarmac. Most of us spent the first half an hour on the truck pulling burrs and thorns out of our clothing, hair and shoes. Some spines were so fine that you could feel them as they hurt, but there was nothing to see. It would take days for them to work themselves out of the skin naturally.

At the border, the getting out of Senegal and the getting stamped into The Gambia was relatively straightforward and the passengers were through relatively quickly; although the paperwork for the truck took a little longer. We had lunch opposite the police station whilst we waited for the truck to clear all its checks, and we were through within two hours.

CHAPTER 5
THE GAMBIA

The Gambia is the smallest country on mainland Africa and is surrounded by Senegal except for its short Atlantic coastline. It is one of only two countries officially recognised by the United Nations as being able to use 'The' for its official country of origin definition. The other country is The Bahamas.

It was originally a Portuguese colony and had trading links with Britain as early as during the reign of Elizabeth I in the sixteenth century. It became part of the British Empire in 1815 with the establishment of Fort James with the aim of establishing a colony. It became a self-governing colony in 1888 and became independent in 1963.

The country is long and thin, stretching along both sides of the Gambia River for over three hundred kilometres, but not more than fifty kilometres at its widest point. There is an urban myth that the boundaries further up the river were decided by the distance that a gunboat could fire from the centre of the river. It is a good story and one that was repeated to me several times, but I could not find any authoritative source to confirm it, other than that the borders were agreed with France at the Treaty of Paris in 1889, but it took another fifteen years for the border markers to be agreed on the ground; mostly due to local resistance to having their traditional tribal areas cut in half by Europeans. The typical battleship of the British navy at the time was the Dreadnought class of ships, whose main armament of twelve inch guns could fire an eight hundred and fifty pound shell only ten kilometres and with the draught of the battleship exceeding the depth of the river, I regret to bust the urban myth but the stories are spurious.

We were on the north side of the country and Banjul; the capital and our campsite were on the southern half. The original settlement was on an island in the river which was called Banjul Island which was renamed in 1816 by Alexander Grant, the British commandant who founded a town here called Bathurst, named after the third Earl of Bathurst who was the Secretary of State for War and the Colonies as a trading post and a base for suppressing the slave trade.

England had banned slave trading throughout the British Empire in 1807 under the Slave Trade Act (but slavery itself was not made illegal until the Slavery Abolition Act of 1833). Slave ships that were intercepted by the Royal Navy's West Africa Squadron were returned to The Gambia and the former slaves were released on MacCarthy Island, two hundred and seventy kilometres up the Gambia River, where they were expected to establish new lives for themselves. It was a military garrison town with little other reason for being, except to reinforce the navy's claim to the area. The island was named after Sir Charles MacCarthy, former Governor General of the British West Africa Territories. It was also a military prison and even today, it is the largest prison in The Gambia. The city of Bathurst was only renamed Banjul in 1973.

The Gambia River dissects the whole country and there are no bridges across the river. We would need to take the ferry to get across from one side to the other. We drove towards the port and went to the weighbridge first. After getting our weight recorded, we moved on to join the queue to get onto the ferry. We were at the head of the queue, in front of the gates, to get into the port. But unbeknown to us, there were already several vehicles queueing ahead of us around the corner, that would be getting onto the next ferry. We were called forward but only to join the end of the queue ahead of us.

A ferry arrived, loaded, and departed without us. The next ferry arrived and we got right to the front, only to be told that we were too heavy for the back of the ferry, and several cars were called forward from behind us and another ferry left without us.

The next ferry was able to take us, and we were waved aboard to our position, somewhere in the middle of the ferry.

It seemed to be a lot of effort to weigh all the vehicles and assign places, based on the weights of the vehicles, but a ferry had sunk in an incident a couple of years previously, and there were many stories of the chaos that ensued with the reduction in ferry capacity leading to long queues and overloading, hence new regulations followed, which were strictly enforced. A new ferry had been delivered just four months previously and everyone was speaking in awe, as now it was so much better than it had been for months since the sinking. It was also a lot faster and people seemed to hope to be able to cross the short stretch of water on the new, clean, fast ferry, but there was a one in four chance of getting onto the new one.

The ferry was crowded with people squeezed onto both the passenger decks and the vehicle decks. There were hawkers walking around the ferry, selling their wares, mostly something to eat or to drink such as frozen yoghurts, chilled soft drinks, fresh fruit, baked cakes, biscuits, plus a few other useful items such as sunglasses, plus a host of other things that one might just want, as an impulse buy, such as trousers, beads or dresses.

We moored at the ferry terminal and the mass of people got off, followed by the vehicles. We drove through the capital to the outskirts and found our campsite at Sukuta Camping. It was a little difficult to find our bearings on our computers and our phones. The spot on the maps recorded for Sukuta Camping was different from that in reality. It was over a kilometre away, so it caused endless confusion regarding how to find the place, and how to get from there to anywhere else. We had to use old fashion common sense, initiative and a sense of direction.

We were dressed in our best to go to the Nigerian embassy to get our visas. The office hours were advertised as nine a.m. to five p.m. but we arrived on time, only to discover that the visa opening hours started at ten a.m. so we had another hour to wait, to read, to chill out, or to get a coffee from one of the ladies who had a stall on the side of the road.

Our applications were initially processed but then to continue the application we would have to go to the bank. The embassy doesn't accept money, so you must go to a local bank, pay the money in to their account, get a receipt, and then return to the embassy to present the receipt with your application.

We had a truck lunch opposite the embassy, whilst we waited for news of our applications. When we checked on the progress of our application and hoping to get our passport back the same day, we were advised that the visa section was due to close at three p.m. and not the five p.m. as advertised, but we got a receipt for depositing our passports, bank details, photos and applications, and we would be required to return in person in two days' time. Therefore, we had some extra time in The Gambia to fill.

We went back to the hostel via the supermarket. The cost of the visas was less than advertised and for some nationalities, it was just a few euros, so everyone was happy to have saved some money, and others had saved hundreds of euros. Therefore, there was an over exuberance of overlanders, and much more alcohol was purchased than necessary, and the evening celebrations started in the mid-afternoon.

We had some free time, as we had to sit around, whilst the embassy processed our documents. So, the next day I walked the three kilometres to the local shops, had a bean sandwich in the market and a haircut. Then, I walked in the other direction but there was nothing of note. I was just filling in time and stretching my legs and seeing what a town in The Gambia looks like. It was also hot, and I was looking for a cold drink, but there were none available, so I headed back to the shade and quiet of the campsite.

We returned to the Nigerian embassy in the afternoon for our final interview, and to collect our passports with the visa stamped inside. Then it was a short trip around the corner to visit the Sierra Leone embassy, to get another visa which they promised would be ready the next day. We returned to the campsite and it was my cook group's turn to cook the evening meal and breakfast.

At last, Kenny had got it. He was up with the rest of the cook group half an hour before breakfast and contributed to getting breakfast ready. But he was slow to get any job finished and he was easily distracted. He would still be eating when everyone else had finished and the kitchen was tidied away, so he rarely pulled his weight by helping and tidying things away. By the time he had finished his breakfast, everything except for his plate and cutlery had been washed and packed away. Noah was still out of his depth. He didn't seem to have any sense of personal space. He would eat his meal standing up, as he had back problems and had found standing more comfortable. Nothing wrong with that, but he was always in the way. The stools were always arranged in a circle around the fire. At the evening meals, there would be additional lights on poles sticking out from the side of the truck, to illuminate the tables where the cooks would be preparing the meal and where it would be served, and people could help themselves to sauces, which would also be on the table.

Noah would stand between the fire and the people sitting in a circle around the fire. If he wasn't standing there, he might stand in front of the table where people wanted to queue to get their food or their selection of sauces. He might move to the other side of the table and stand in front of the lights, and therefore cast a shadow over the circle of stools, and people would have to peer into the darkness to see what they were doing. But at least he now joined in cleaning some of the kitchen things, as well as his own things.

But I always avoided eating near him. He ate with his mouth open, and it is unpleasant to see anyone chewing their food; a bit like watching a washing machine churn its load around. He would also talk at the same time, and you might get a splattering of partly chewed food. I had good table manners drilled into me as a child and I find bad manners particularly offensive. I have dumped girlfriends for nothing more than not eating with their mouths closed.

We were waiting for a call from the embassy, so that we could go and collect our passports. People filled in the time doing laundry, reading or walking around the campsite, but not going far just in case the embassy wanted to see each of us in person. It was lunchtime and still there was no news from the embassy. We got the call from them in the late afternoon. We didn't need to all turn up in person, so Kim got a taxi and collected all our passports and then we were free to do what we liked.

We had a plan to leave our current campsite and head east upriver to an eco-lodge and campsite on the banks of the Gambia River. Once we had left the suburbs, there was a lot less traffic. There were frequent police checks, although most of the chat was friendly, welcoming us to The Gambia and wanting to know where we were going, and wishing us a good and a safe journey.

For the last two hours of the journey, there was hardly any traffic, just an occasional tractor or a donkey pulling a cart. We turned off the main road and followed a side road down to the river and thence to the Tendaba Eco camp site and lodge. We camped on the beach between the eco-lodge and the river. There were no upgrades available as the lodge was hosting a last night dinner for a hundred and twenty- strong student party, so it was going to be crowded at the bar that night.

There were various tours on offer such as boat rides to see the birds and a safari in an open truck to see the wildlife, or of course, the opportunity to chill out and do nothing and read next to the pool. I went for a walk by myself through the forest to the next village. The track was deserted and other than a few pedestrians and cyclists, I saw only one vehicle all morning, which was the time it took me to get to the next village. It wasn't that far but I did take a few diversions to investigate side turnings and to take photos of wildlife. But my number one aim was to get a photo of a large termite mound.

I saw some warthogs scurrying through the undergrowth not far from the track. I saw a monkey scamper across the road. There were lots of birds singing and flying through the trees, but it was hard to see any of them clearly, until they broke cover and flew into the open, over the road.

I crossed a dam that was part of an internationally funded project to counter salt intrusion and to rehabilitate dozens of hectares of rice fields, and to preserve a small area of mangrove swamp. Down a side turning, I came across a peanut oil processing plant built on a cliff overlooking the river. Local farmers would bring their groundnuts here to be processed and the resultant oil was taken away by river tanker, which is loaded directly from the cliff top at the edge of the facility.

Back at the eco-lodge, one group left, and another arrived. The hundred and twenty students left in the morning, but another group arrived in the afternoon; nearly all of them, including the teachers, wearing the same brightly multi-coloured tee-shirts with their names on the back.

They were singing and partying, banging sticks together and playing several pairs of bongo drums from after dinner, well into the night, and I was lying in my tent awake, listening to it, for what seemed like most of the night.

We had an early breakfast to allow those going on an early morning boat cruise time to have breakfast and then leave. I went for another walk along some paths that I had not walked along the day before. There were no wildlife encounters and I returned to the camp for a swim to cool off before lunch, and our departure back towards Banjul.

We stopped en route to allow the next cook groups to shop, and then we were back at our familiar campground of Sukuta Camping. But all was not well at the campsite. Apparently, their Wi-Fi had had a problem the day we had left. The engineer that came to fix it claimed that someone had corrupted the security protocols and had hacked into the network and the finger was pointed at us.

I don't understand why a group of travellers would bother to hack into the campsite's Wi-Fi, when we had access to it anyway, but that is what the engineer had told the proprietors. They had a business to run and therefore they had reset the password and would not allow us to join the network. If someone was bright enough to hack into the system, then not giving us the password would not protect the system. Either way, they had a business to run and wanted to protect their network, but I wanted the internet, so I went to find another hotel with Wi-Fi.

I walked out of the campsite before breakfast the next morning and sought out a hotel. I had a few requirements – Wi-Fi that worked, a beach front location, a pool to swim in, and fish on the menu, plus not located too far from the campsite, as I would have to get back to re-join the group before they left on the last morning. Was I asking too much?

I walked to the roundabout known as the Turntable, and I was intrigued as to how it had got its name. I couldn't find any reference to any railway ever being built here which was my first guess as to why it was called the Turntable. I tried researching trams but with no luck, so it got its name for reasons unknown and lost over time.

I walked further down the road to where I had seen a Sheraton Hotel marked on a map on the internet. It was a pointless walk, as the hotel was not at the allotted location. It was just like the campsite which appears at a different location on Google maps than it does in reality. I tried the internet café so I could search for a hotel. However, the internet was down, and so I reverted to an old but tried and tested method and asked passing locals for directions.

I walked along the beachfront and looked for likely candidates that fitted my requirements. I found Leo's which was where Mike stayed a few nights before as it had just six rooms but no swimming pool, so I walked on.

There were other potentials but none that quite fitted the bill. For instance, the Beach View Hotel had Wi-Fi, a pool, and was beachfront but there was a feeble menu but there was a good restaurant next door. The two issues were that I couldn't book in as the man who did the bookings only came on duty after lunch, and they didn't know if the internet was available in the rooms or at the bar. The only place it was available for certain was in reception, but as it was not working at the time, neither they nor I could check whether there was internet elsewhere in the hotel.

The Ocean Spa Resort was a lovely place with armed guards at the entrances, beautiful grounds and high security. I was questioned and my bags x-rayed before I was allowed in. It fitted most of my requirements, but again, they couldn't tell me about the internet and the pool was being repaired, and so it was out of use.

Another hotel fitted all the requirements (except the internet as it was still off, but they assured me that it worked well everywhere in the hotel), and it wasn't expensive, but it had just one major drawback. It had a swimming pool so, technically it fitted the bill, but it was shaded by several large trees and had a lot of insects, leaves and other things in it, but it didn't put me off as much as the fact that it was so dirty that I couldn't see the bottom.

Whilst walking along the beach front I came across two military Toyota pickups with several armed soldiers on patrol. They all had ECOWAS written across the back of their uniforms. This is the Economic Community of West Africa States. It was established in 1975 to promote self-sufficiency of member states by creating a large trading bloc, with a full economic and trading union. There are fifteen-member states with a combined population of 350 million.

There are two sub blocs. One is the West African Economic and Monetary Union established in 1994. It had eight members, mainly French speaking countries who share a customs and currency union. It is also known by its French acronym, UEMOA. They all use the CFA franc as currency (pronounced Ceefa). It is pegged to the euro and guaranteed by the French Treasury.

The other sub bloc is the West African Monetary Zone (WAMZ) which was established in 2000. It has six mainly English-speaking countries, who plan to work towards adopting their own common currency, the eco.

ECOWAS also has a peacekeeping force which is used at times of political and social unrest. It intervened in the Ivory Coast, in Guinea-Bissau in 2003 and in The Gambia in 2017. There were presidential elections there in 2016. Yahya Jammeh first came to power in a bloodless coup in 1994 and won his first presidential election in 1996. He was re-elected several times but lost the 2016 elections to Adama Barrow. He originally said that he would stand down, but then he changed his mind, and said that he didn't recognise the elections. This sparked a constitutional crisis, unrest and ECOWAS intervention. Yahya Jammeh went into exile and Adama Barrow became president but requested that the ECOWAS troops remain to maintain peace. The troops that I had come across were Nigerian.

I moved further along the beach front and came to a hotel whose gardens faced the beach and it was virtually empty of people. This was the Kumaisa Beach Hotel whose main building was undergoing a major refurbishment, so it had no guests in residence. But it had a bar, a varied menu, a small pool, their internet was working and due to the lack of other guests, I might be the only person on the Wi-Fi so the bandwidth would not be under strain with dozens of users.

It was ideal, and I spent the rest of the day there swimming, reading and relaxing. All the staff were still working but with no guests, the staff to customer ratio was excellent, and the service was excellent also. I had several chats with the bar staff, the waiters and the security guards.

After a long hot day, I had my last swim to cool off, and packed away my things. I had used all the internet that I needed, and I said goodbye to the staff, as I returned to my campsite, having completed all the jobs that I needed to do. But as is sometimes the case, I forgot to send an email to my publisher that I had spent days in deciding the exact wording, but having had all day to create it, I had forgotten to hit the send button, and it only struck me as I was walking back to the campsite.

I revisited the Kumaisa Beach Hotel several times before it was time to move on. We stopped at the Turntable for some shopping. The same group of ECOWAS peacekeepers were patrolling at the Turntable, and I nodded in recognition as I walked past them. Kim collected our passports for us, from the Sierra Leone embassy and we left The Gambia for Senegal.

The border crossing was painless, except that it still took a couple of hours to clear all the formalities. We headed south through more savannah, but I was certain that the trees were growing more closely together, and that the undergrowth was greener. We passed through some low-lying areas, with occasional salt marshes. The road was poor in places as it was built on raised banks of sand, and it was unstable with the sides deteriorating, and with large holes in the tarmac surface. Several former ferry crossings along the road had been replaced with bridges, although the old landing stages were still there, and there were ghost towns of abandoned trader's stalls and huts, scattered about the former landing points.

We eventually crossed the last large stretch of water and entered Ziguinchor on the Casamance River. It has a large stadium which dominates the city. It claims to be the second largest city in Senegal and its suburbs are expanding at a rapid rate. It struggles with Touba to claim the accolade of being the second largest city in the country, as they are of similar size, but the results of another census will decide which is the larger of the two, but the next census is overdue. Having passed through both, I would put my money on Touba being the larger of the two.

Ziguinchor was founded by the Portuguese in 1645. The king of the area was friendly towards the Portuguese, and so they established a trading post to trade here. It became a large slave trading centre with the locals providing slaves from the hinterland. With the ending of the slave trade, many of the traders moved away and the Portuguese handed over the area to the French, under the terms of the Berlin Conference in 1886. The French government encouraged groundnut production which became a major export, including both the nuts and the oil that it produced. Groundnuts overtook the local rice production farming, with cheaper imports of rice coming from French Indochina.

It was a lovely campsite just past the stadium and we had it to ourselves. It was fenced, with soft sand, plenty of shade from trees, palms, and bougainvillea and both Western toilets and showers. There was no hot water but there was an ample supply of ambient water with privacy and after a hot day, a cool shower can be heaven. The next morning, we stopped off at the Guinea-Bissau embassy which was a ten-minute drive from the camp site. They were very efficient, and they had completed the first four visas within ten minutes. The rest of the morning was free for us to explore Zuguinchor.

I walked past the West African University and the port before I arrived in the centre of town. It was an interesting place but other than a few colonial buildings in need of some renovation, there was little to see. I was happy that when our time to leave arrived, I would not feel that I had missed anything.

I got my secret Santa present for Mat. I was looking for inspiration and had found a child's plastic toy scimitar. Mat had a large bushy beard and wherever he went in Morocco and Mauritania, the locals would call out Ali Baba and wave, so a toy scimitar would complement the image. However, I was in another shop and there were Santa hats and his beard would be a natural accompaniment, and therefore I got him the Santa hat instead. He always wore a hat, but I was sure that he would not wear the Santa hat, but it was just for a bit of fun.

We left Zuguinchor and we headed south towards the border. It should have been a simple affair, but it still took a few hours. We were asked to get off the truck and then asked to return to the checkpoint with our bags. Then we were told to go back and another official told us to stand still. Also, the officials didn't all wear uniforms, so it was difficult to distinguish who was in a position of authority and who was just a hanger on or a local, who was trying to be helpful, but in fact was making the experience even more chaotic by pointing this way and that. We moved from the front of the office to the side and back again. We took our day packs and some tents and stood in front of the check point and still they couldn't decide what to do with us.

Eventually I think that they got tired of us being in the way, and they really didn't want the job of searching our bags, so they told us to get back on the truck, and eventually, we and the truck got through all the requirements and were stamped into Guinea-Bissau.

CHAPTER 6
GUINEA-BISSAU

The scenery hadn't really changed but after the border it was just flatter savannah and the occasional salt marsh, as we drove east, parallel to the shore line of a tidal river. We followed the Cacheu River inland, catching glimpses of the river through the trees.

The Cape Verde Islands just off the coast had become a colony in 1456 so it was natural that Guinea-Bissau being the nearby mainland to the islands would also come under Portuguese influence from the late fifteenth century. The initial impetus for exploration came from the Portuguese crown who wanted to discover the source of the gold and slave trades, which were dominated by Moroccan traders.

The Portuguese colonisers of the area were confined to coastal settlements and the inland tribes restricted Portuguese moves into their territory but were happy to trade. They didn't have much to trade, but they did have neighbouring tribes and so they traded slaves, plus some ivory for goods. It was known as The Slave Coast, as it provided many of the slaves to be shipped to the Americas. More than a hundred and fifty thousand slaves were transported from these shores before 1500; firstly to work in the Cape Verde Islands and later to South America, adding to the more than twelve to twenty million people trafficked across the Atlantic.

An armed rebellion against the Portuguese started in 1956 by the African Party for Independence of Guinea and Cape Verde Islands (PAIGC) led by Amilcar Cabral. They were very successful in controlling much of the country with support from Russia, China and Cuba and left leaning African states. After a long and bloody struggle, independence was achieved in 1973.

The country was formerly called Guinea, but the name of the capital was added at independence, to distinguish it from French Guinea next door which changed its name to Guinea, when it became independent in 1958. It is a poor country. In fact, it is one of the poorest twenty-five countries in the world, and only four of the poorest countries are not in Africa. Why are so many of the poorest countries on the African continent? Is it a result of the history of colonialism, local culture, trading links, politics, geography, climate or some other effect? Probably a bit of each, but other countries have faced difficulties and still developed stable governments and growing economies.

Guinea-Bissau is the eleventh poorest country with a GDP per capita of just USD1,491. Averages conceal an even greater inequality, and two thirds of the population are below the poverty line. Guinea next door is even poorer in ninth position, at USD1,388. I would be passing through many of the poorest but not the poorest which is the Central African Republic with a GDP per capita of just USD639.

Guinea-Bissau is a country with a history of instability. No president has ever served his full five-year term. An ECOWAS peacekeeping operation was carried out in 2012. There was a failed coup in 2011, and presidential elections were held in 2012. Before the second round of voting could occur, there was another military coup. Both leading presidential candidates were arrested, and the third candidate led an interim government. Unrest and instability are also due to the country being a transhipment point for drugs and the corruption that is associated with lawlessness, drugs and bribes.

The official language is Portuguese but only fourteen percent of the population speak it as a first language. But forty-four percent of the population speak a Portuguese creole, and more speak it as a second language, but the majority of the population speaks local African languages.

We continued to drive parallel to the river to Ingoré, where we turned south to cross two major rivers, passing through Sao Vincente, almost to the outskirts of the capital, Bissau, before turning east to cross the northern areas of the country, to get towards the border with Guinea Conakry.

It was getting late in the afternoon, but we passed a quarry and quick as a flash, it was time to check it out for a bush camp. We turned off the main road and bumped along a rough track into the quarry. It was still being used and the aggregate was being extracted by hand, using just picks, shovels and various sizes of sieves as graders. There were a couple of workers sitting on the ground near the entrance, but they just stared at us as we passed.

We found a sheltered spot some way away from the road and we started to cook dinner. As the sun went down, we set up our tents and sat around the fire. The two locals that had seen us enter the quarry had come over to see what was happening. It is rare that you can do anything in Africa without somebody noticing, and telling someone else, and for there to be a group of locals turning up within a few minutes. Eventually the two who had watched from a distance had grown bolder and had moved closer. When they were within talking distance, I gave a friendly greeting and one of them replied. They both lived nearby and worked in the quarry. They worked according to the orders received for aggregate, between four and twelve hours a day, five to six days a week.

They spoke a local language or Portuguese. Luis was Portuguese, but we were wary of demonstrating that we were able to converse fluently, so he stayed in the back ground and we used a mixture of Spanish, French and English to chat. Plus of course for those with smart phones and power, you could tap a question into the phone for our new friends to tap in their answers.

We were up early and drove to Gabu. All the way, the red dust thrown up from the roads covered the leaves of the trees and turned them red. However, the farmhouses seemed to be reproductions of one another. Each had a large corrugated iron roof with a veranda running around all four sides, and a generous overhang to provide shade. Without exception, they were all single storey, built of blocks and often had a little fenced compound created by driving branches end first into the soil, to keep livestock away.

We arrived in Gabu in the early afternoon. It used to be an important place and the regional capital, but since the civil war, it has become just a small town with a market, but vibrant, as only African villages and towns can be, with lots of people, bright colours, lots of talking and the women wearing colourful dresses with loads balanced on their heads. Added to the rainbow of colours were the fruits, vegetables, clothes, shoes and everything else for sale on stalls in the open.

But Gabu was also the end of the good tarmac road. The tarmac road led to a bridge over a small river and from there it was a very bumpy rough road with more potholes than road. It was seventy-eight kilometres to the border, and once upon a time, this was a tarmac road, but it had deteriorated over time, and had not been repaired so the edges were eroded. What little traffic there was had torn up the surface of the tarmac, and every passing vehicle weakened the edges of the potholes and made them a little wider and deeper. It had not had any maintenance for decades, and there were huge potholes in the tarmac where small holes had joined up to make a large hole or trench. Often, it was easier and more comfortable to drive on the hard sand and gravel at the edge of the road.

There were farmhouses and small settlements all along the road, out of town, and well into the depths of the savannah that surrounded the town. The road got progressively worse as it stretched away from the last town in Guinea-Bissau. We were creating a great sandstorm of red dust as we went past. The trees at the side of the road were covered in the red dust and they would only get a washing off at the start of the rainy season. We were making barely twenty kilometres per hour, and it took the rest of the afternoon to get near to the border. There were so many farmhouses and villages that it was going to be difficult to find a bush camp as just where one village finished, then another began.

It was just an hour before sunset when we passed a quarry that had been used to produce the aggregate needed for the road.

Gareth braked hard and backed up and this was to be our bush camp. There was a village just a couple of hundred metres back down the road, and it was inevitable that a group of youngsters came to watch and converse with us in several languages.

It was a good campsite but there were some huts beyond the rim of the quarry and there were some locals in the bushes nearby having a barbecue. We could see the smoke and hear the voices, but we couldn't see any people. There was some bush cover but finding somewhere for a poo in privacy was going to be difficult.

We started a fire and a crowd soon formed. Firstly, it was just a few children but as they were joined by their friends, there was more giggling and pointing. Older sisters held hands with younger siblings. Some of the younger children hid behind older brothers, with just their heads showing. Girls giggled behind hands cupped over their mouths. The bigger children clutched mobile phones, or the distinctive shape of a phone bulged in pockets. They soon lost interest and one by one, left us. A few adults walked past, taking a short cut through the quarry to reach their huts on the far side of the quarry, but unlike the children, they seemed to show no interest. They would return a greeting, but they didn't stop to look or to chat.

The meal that evening was pasta bolognaise, and the cooks used the soya mince from the truck. I don't usually eat soya mince, so I had no idea what to expect, but it was so salty that everyone agreed that it was so unpleasant as to be disgusting.

In the morning, we were watched by several locals, but no children, as they were off to school, walking past the entrance to the quarry and looking and waving, but not stopping. There were several dead trees around and we needed more firewood. The thinner branches had already been scavenged, but the thicker heavier trunks had been left as they were too big. We got the chain saw out, to cut some good quality hard wood logs. The cut sections needed to be split, to be ready for the fire, but we would do that in the next camp. Mat often did the splitting, as he was good at it and enjoyed doing it. We just packed the sawn pieces straight into the locker.

Back on the rough 'road', just twelve kilometres took an hour, as it was so bad and it got even worse, and after the last settlement, it deteriorated to just a rutted track. We were stamped out of Guinea-Bissau by an official sitting on the veranda of a single small mud hut, and drove along a road that was no more than a dirt track, with a rivulet down the centre and we reached the Guinea border station which was another small mud hut next to the dirt track, that probably hadn't seen any traffic for the past six months.

CHAPTER 7
GUINEA CONAKRY

We were through in under forty minutes, which was a record for African border crossings, but Kim had printed out a list of names, passport numbers, nationalities, our schedule and details of the next place that we would be staying, so that they had all the information that they wanted. They could write it into their book in their own time, and we would not be delayed.

We call the country Guinea but many people talking about West Africa call it Guinea Conakry, Conakry being the capital, in order to distinguish it from Guinea-Bissau next door, or Equatorial Guinea further along the coast. It was part of several African kingdoms in the area, until French colonial expansion in the mid-nineteenth century extended their influence inland. It became a colony in 1898 after local armed resistance was defeated. French is the official language, but there are twenty-four other languages spoken in the country.

The French government, led by Charles de Gaulle, made it clear that French colonies could choose either autonomy within a French community or independence. It was the start of the granting of independence to many African colonies, with Britain following suit in the 1960s. The Dutch had trading interests but no colonies, concentrating on the Caribbean and the Far East. The Spanish only had two colonies, Western Sahara and Equatorial Guinea. The Germans had been stripped of their colonies after the First World War. Portugal held on to her colonies for another decade before a change of government and policy at home started the independence movement in former Portuguese colonies.

Of the two choices facing Guinea, it chose independence, which it achieved in 1958, led by Ahmed Sekou Toure and his

Democratic Party of Guinea (DPG). In 1960, Toure declared that there was only one party, his DPG, and he ruled the country for the next twenty-four years, as an autocrat, following his version of African socialism. Like many one-party systems, the government became intolerant of dissent and thousands were imprisoned, tortured and murdered. This was to be a common experience of many newly independent countries, where newly installed governments became led by one man, who held onto power for as long as he could. Many became corrupt wanting power for prestige, influence and wealth, crushing opposition and any checks on their grip on power. They ruled for their own benefit, rather than for the benefit of the nation.

The governments have changed but the political and social unrest have not ceased. There have been elections, but outcomes are disputed, and there are still plenty of problems.

It is a poor country, but they have resources. Over sixty percent of their exports is bauxite, the ore for making aluminium, and the deposits represent half of the world's known bauxite reserves. There are large deposits of iron ore. There are gold and diamond deposits. There are yet unverified quantities of uranium; but the poor infrastructure, corruption, political uncertainty and past problems deter large scale investment. Africa is crying out for development, but things move slowly in Africa. It seems that to get anything done, you need to offer a bribe. Then things happen and overseas financial investigators get involved and discover bribery and corruption, and projects are halted, and licences rescinded or funding halted.

Only fifty-two percent of Guinean males are literate (thirty percent are females) and primary school attendance is only forty percent of eligible children. Girls are especially prone to being held back from going to school, being forced to help with domestic chores, instead. The country is in the top five countries that have the highest incidence of child marriages.

The average sub Saharan African adult remains below the poverty line, poorly educated, with little prospects, superstitious following tradition and witch doctors, rather than scientifically proven options, is subject to failed health care systems, corrupt officials and the areas are badly governed. The people's frustrations are sometimes voiced but are not acted upon or remain unheard and the people are often subject to violent repression by security forces who are loyal to the ruling elite, who ensure that they are paid well, to retain that loyalty.

Those in power can shower favours on others and get rich from corruption and the exercise of power. They exercise power more for their own ends than for the good of the nation that they rule, without accountability. Meanwhile, most of the population is ignored. Martin Meredith's book titled 'The State of Africa' details much of the history of African states following independence, which most of the group read whilst on the trip, and it gives a fascinating insight into African politics. Some of the details differed between countries. but the theme was the same and was all too often repeated from country to country.

The road from the border post was also just a rough track and we bumped along at less than twenty kilometres per hour. We were passing alongside a massive cliff face that towered above us for hour after hour, the result of some massive faulting in the earth's crust. We passed a few farms, and later through several villages. The locals smiled and waved as we passed, and we returned their greetings.

We bumped along for more than three hours before we reached the town of Koundara in the very north of the country. It was prayer time and the banks were closed. We had to wander around town aimlessly, trying to find somewhere to change money, somewhere to throw our accumulated rubbish and somewhere to find some water. Therefore, different groups were assigned different tasks, while also doing their personal shopping. Gareth got a moto taxi, a chap with a motor bike acting like a taxi, to take him and some tents that needed mending to find a man who had an industrial sewing machine, to sew up the canvas and to repair some zips. The same chap also took him to the local ice merchant, so that we had ice for the large ice boxes, to keep the food and drinks cool.

What most people wanted was time to change money and to get SIM cards. The banks were closed but I found a money changer, after asking around the market. Most of the group went to the same phone shop and there was soon a queue. We were an hour late leaving there, and some people didn't have the right data package that they thought they had bought.

Another major issue was the search for beer, which was difficult and can often be fruitless and is always a challenge in a Muslim country. More than eighty-five percent of the population in Guinea are Muslim. I wrote down what people wanted and got a moto taxi; the same chap who had taken Gareth to get the tents repaired. He took me straight out of town and up what seemed to be a dead end. He turned through some gates and stopped. We walked through a door with a net curtain hanging over it, into a dark, dirty room lined with tables and benches. There were empty bottles and beer cans on the tables and on the floor. It smelt of stale beer and body odour. At one end of the room was a doorway with another table pushed across the opening.

There were two girls asleep on the benches. He roused one of them, and she slipped under the table pushed against the doorway and disappeared down the hallway. She returned a little later with three types of beer. I made my selections from what people had ordered and paid the bill. I climbed onto the back of the motorbike and balanced the selection of beers on my lap and held on tight, with one hand on to the stack of beer cans between me and the driver, with the other hand holding on to the edge of the seat. I am not a natural motor bike passenger, and I am nervous riding pillion, but he was a good driver and I got back to the truck with the goods, 'shaken' over the rough road 'but not stirred.'

The afternoon drive was a pleasure. After the rough tracks, there was a smooth well maintained road leading out of Koundara. It had no potholes. There were bright white lines down the middle and the sides. There were clear signs, bollards and crash barriers on corners, and where there were steep drops at the side of the road.

We found a good bush camp off the road and into the forest. The ground was flat, and there was plenty of wood, but there was a lot of laterite everywhere. It becomes rock hard and makes driving pegs in or digging a hole for your 'business' difficult.

During the night, we were moved on, by some of the local villagers who had come out to check on us. They were friendly, but they didn't want us camping just there and they wanted us to move on. There was a language issue, and I didn't understand why they didn't want us just there, but the meaning was clear. We didn't want to get involved with police and landowners, so we packed up in the dark, and drove on a few kilometres.

The alternative camp site was a rocky barren area full of sharp-edged lumps of laterite. Much of the area had suffered from fires and the grass had been burnt and just left black ash. There were few trees, as the ground is typically too hard for them to get established and throw down deep enough roots in the wet season to survive through the next dry season, with its merciless heat and wildfires.

It wasn't a good bush camp, as there was no cover for privacy and the recently burnt undergrowth had left a lot of ash that covered our tents, shoes and legs. We got back on the road, but the good tarmac finished abruptly, and the road turned to red dust again. As we drove, we threw up great clouds of red dust which coated the back of the truck and the roadside vegetation. We passed through some forest and then the road started to climb up into the mountains, snaking its way across some slopes as it went deeper into the hills.

There were bromeliads and bamboos by the side of the road, but they were covered in red dust and the few bits of green that could be seen didn't suggest that they were in the best of health. We made slow progress as the track was very rutted and snaked its way across slopes, around valleys and over ravines. There wasn't much traffic but there were people. There were women carrying bundles of clothes or firewood on their heads, and children in groups of four or five carrying large bundles of hay on their heads, back to their village hidden somewhere in the jungle.

We were moving into the mountains and there were valleys to cross, mountains to negotiate and the sometimes-thick forest of the Fouta Djallon plateau, which gave shade but also obscured the views. There were many potential viewpoints for great views as the track curved around a hillside, overlooking a wide valley but it was hot and we welcomed the breeze coming in through the windows as we drove, so we didn't stop too often.

This highland area captures much of the rain from the Atlantic and it is the source of several major rivers such as the Gambia and Senegal Rivers which we had crossed earlier. The Tinkisso River, a major tributary of the Niger, has its source here, which flows north in a great arc through Mali, Niger, to reach the sea on the shores of Nigeria. The Nunez and Pongo Rivers also have their sources here, and are major rivers flowing through Guinea to the Atlantic. Sir George Collier was the Commodore of the British West Africa Squadron between 1818 and 1821, and he listed seventy-six families who were engaged in the slave trade along the Pongo River as it was a major conduit for slave caravans coming from the interior down to the coast. Therefore, he sent patrols along this and other rivers in the area, to curb the slave trade.

Then, around a corner, the tarmac started again, abruptly. It was the same smooth black surface of a recently laid road with white lines and crash barriers. It restarted as abruptly as it had stopped three hours before, yet only some forty kilometres away.

Although one of the poorest countries, Guinea Conakry is also one of the proudest in West Africa. Its people have stood together and have survived the difficult post-colonial era of independence, without resorting to tribal conflicts or extensive inter-tribal civil war. They were the first colony to gain independence from their French colonial overlords, and they stated that they preferred 'freedom in poverty than prosperity in chains'.

The road dipped as we drove through the spectacular tropical forests to cross a river, the first one we had seen for several days, and having been bush camping for several nights, we stopped for a swim. There were several cataracts and pools in between, and it was an opportunity to soak off some of the dirt. Many of us had been wearing sandals and the combination of DEET, the red dust and the ashes from fires had made our feet filthy. We splashed about and soaked our feet in the river. It wasn't deep enough to swim, but it did take some of the dirt off.

We moved on to Lafou and to Labe, where we stocked up with Christmas drinks, largely beer and red wine in the absence of any white wine. Then we drove to the Tata Hotel to camp in their grounds. We spent the morning in Labe doing Christmas shopping and whatever personal shopping we needed to do. We split into groups to get certain items. The cook group still had to buy for an evening meal but other pairs were tasked to find a couple of trays of eggs, blocks of ice, salad, and kilos of potatoes for mash and roast potatoes. Sarah took on the task of getting ingredients for the vegetarians' Christmas meal.

We had everything that we needed and set off to leave Labe. We drove on to Kinkon Waterfalls. There is a dam which provides drinking water for the town and a hydroelectric power station and it's something of value, as it is both a park and a military area, to protect the infrastructure. We negotiated a price of thirty thousand Guinean Francs, about three Euros each, to enter the park and camp for two nights.

The park has a gorge where two rivers meet, and it is a recommended swimming spot. Therefore, we parked the truck and walked down to the swimming hole. It was also an opportunity to wash our clothes and ourselves, and to have a soak, to try and get some more of the ingrained dust out of our hair and our clothes and to freshen up.

The campsite had once been savannah, but there had been some bush fires and whilst there were some trees left standing, the ground was devoid of undergrowth and was just a mass of black ash. Bush fires burn quickly through the tall standing grasses but move on equally quickly. They generate enough heat for long enough to start branches and trees burning. The flames whip up in the wind but move on quickly. Therefore, some of the upper leaves and branches on the larger bushes and trees can survive, ready to grow when the next rainy season starts.

This has an unexpected result, as where the tall grasses have been trodden down on a path, the path is still covered with horizontal unburnt grasses but they are surrounded by black ash. Therefore, there are ribbons of trodden down dried grasses marking the paths, surrounded by huge areas of black ash.

It was Christmas Eve and I was in the cook group, with Sarah and Kenny and served corn beef hash for the meat eaters and a bean salad for the vegetarians. In the morning it was Happy Christmas everyone! It was pancakes for breakfast plus chocolates carefully hoarded all the way from England two months before. It was only mid-morning, but we had our secret Santa gift giving session.

Gadget man Stefano had a squeezy bottle of Nutella. Mat who thinks of Christmas like scrooge and calls it humbug, got his Christmas Santa hat, so he joined in the spirit of Christmas and put it on, but not quite as predicted back in Senegal when I bought it, he didn't take it off, but put his own hat back on top of it. By late morning there was no trace of the Santa hat, only one of his usual range of hats.

Martin got his own private beer cooler, with space for six beer cans but there were only two beer cans in it. There were supposed to have been six, but the others got drunk by mistake. I got a handheld mirror since I was always trying to shave at breakfast with a shard of mirror.

Then there was time for an early afternoon swim, an excellent opportunity for taking a wash and for doing laundry. We tried washing out feet again, but with so much dust and ash around, once you had washed your feet, they would be dirty and as black as before when you got back to camp.

The Christmas meal started with aperitifs and a range of hors d'oeuvres with mince pies (again carefully hoarded from England), Christmas cake, several types of sausages, including salami and smoked sausage, cheese for the vegetarians, and a serrano ham from Spain. It was then that we realized that we had smuggled pork products through Mauritania, so we were lucky that we hadn't been searched too thoroughly.

Then we had the cooked chicken instead of turkey. There were dips, mash potatoes, hummus, salads and bean salad. Lunch carried on into the evening and some people drifted away for a swim or for an after-lunch walk, to settle the stomach. Others just carried on partying into the evening.

After so much celebrating the night before, we had a late start and had time for a swim before setting off. Then it was a forty-minute bumpy ride back to the tarmac, and then on to Pita.

We needed petrol, water, and ice plus beers. The Total petrol station business model meant that they often had all these plus clean functional toilets and an outside tap to fill up the jerry cans, so we stopped at the first one and we fanned out in small groups to get the requisites. Stops at Total garage petrol stations had become almost de rigueur on the trip. We knew that they had electricity to operate the pumps. That meant that they also had electricity to have freezer cabinets for ice creams, often ice if they had a clean water supply, and there would be cold drinks cabinets.

They were only too happy to help, so we filled up fifteen jerry cans of water, and in return, we emptied their drinks cabinet of cold beers, several cartons of wine and some spirits, plus most of their supply of Pringles. The girl in the shop was only too happy to help, and she was able to practice both her French and her English, perhaps not enough to have an in-depth conversation, but enough to complete the transaction. Of course, I complicated her on her knowledge of both languages as both would be second or third languages for her, and she was studying to improve her fluency.

We drove out of the petrol station and down the road to another waterfall site. Just a few kilometres out of town we turned off the tarmac main road and bumped along another dusty track, throwing up great clouds of dust.

We stopped under a large tree and had a truck lunch of leftovers from Christmas lunch. We were a constant source of interest to passing children, on their way back from school. One child was walking by herself and she stopped and watched us from fifty metres away, for fifteen minutes until an adult that she obviously knew, and his daughter came along the road and they walked past in a group of three. We smiled and waved, and she coyly waved back, but the adult spoke enough French to welcome us to his country.

Later, we were accosted by several men. We needed guides and it was compulsory for tourists to have a guide and for a group of our size, we needed two guides. Other men turned up, and there was a lot of shouting. We couldn't speak fluently to all of the men, as only a few of the locals spoke French or English; but eventually we hired two guides. One got in the cab and the other held onto the outside.

Three others also tagged along, hanging onto the back of the truck, but we had to stop to tell them to get off. It is charitable and an often practised option to give locals a lift hanging onto the back, but as Europeans, we had health and safety issues, and legal compensation issues. They wouldn't appreciate the issues and they complained about it, but our local guide and fixer made sure that there were no freeloading passengers, and we continued.

We arrived at the Kambadaga waterfalls. Our guides had taken us to the top of the falls, and we had some time to walk around the river and to gaze over the gorge below. There was a flimsy rope bridge, some cascades leading down to the waterfall, and a view from the top of the waterfall down the gorge.

I was disappointed, as I wanted to see the waterfall from the bottom and look up at its majesty. There was also the issue of the guides, as we had employed two, but others had appeared from nowhere, and did their best to persuade us to take them along, as additional guides. Their tactic was to walk with tourists and then claim that they had guided us, and I was concerned that they would all want to be paid, so I purposely ignored them and took a different route.

A kilometre back along the track was a turnoff, and I walked back to it. I had passed one track leaving the road, but it just didn't seem right, so I ignored it and continued up the track. It was uphill, rough ground and hot and dusty and walking into the sun. At the top of a rise was a small path off to the left, and I followed it, and met Mike as he was returning from the spot that I was seeking, and he confirmed that I was on the correct path. It virtually doubled back, parallel to our route, but came out on the cliffs above the gorge, and it was a full-frontal view of the waterfall, a two-tiered drop of eighty metres and twenty metres.

Then I went back to the river and I had a swim with a few of the others. I washed my clothes first, and then left them in the sun to dry, as I went for another swim. I saw some of the others downstream and I walked down to join them but arrived just as they were getting out. I walked back to the truck, and we went back up the track and dropped our guides off at their village and continued the hour's drive back to the main road.

Along the main road, the tropical jungle gave way to grass savannah; a plain full of tall grasses, so plenty of space but little to hide the whole squatting body. So, when it came to a toilet stop, it was boys to one side, and girls to the other.

By the time we got to Dabala, several of us needed to exchange more money. We would be camping in the grounds of a local three-star hotel for a few days. Although some people did get an upgrade. Martin did that, as he always did, whenever he could, as did Noodles and Dazzle. I opted to camp and did little in camp other than to sweep out the truck and wash the floor and then sit back and relax.

I found the local money changer by asking a lot of people. I asked several of the locals and one eventually gave me directions, but it was not an easy route. He saw me struggling to remember the number of lefts and rights, so he asked two young lads, his son and his best friend, to take me there. They took me on a tour through the local market to a small office, in a row of shops on the far side of the market. They both refused a small tip in cash, so we went to a local street stall, and I bought them both a soft drink for their efforts.

Back at the money changers, he offered me a good rate, so I immediately changed quite a lot more than I needed, but I was taking advantage of the best rate that I had come across for several days.

After driving through the mountains and through Momou, we crossed a bridge and stopped at the back of a long line of traffic. Cars were going past in both directions, but the lorries were all parked at the side of the road, their engines off, and their drivers sitting in the shade of some trees, by the side of the road.

We didn't know what the problem was, so I walked up the road to see. A lorry had broken down and had pulled over to the side of the road. Another lorry had pulled out into the middle of the road to pass it, on a bend going uphill, and had also broken down in the middle of the road. A heavily laden car had tried to pass on the steeply sloping verge, but it was top heavy and the slope down from the road to the gutter was so steep that it had fallen over onto its side.

Only cars could squeeze around the vehicles to get past. But no one wanted to give way, so each driver was shouting at the other drivers to back up and to let them pass. The drivers of the broken-down lorries had tinkered with their vehicles to no avail and were waiting for a tow truck to rescue them. The other lorry drivers could only sit and watch and wait for the road to be cleared, which it would be, but being Africa, it would take time.

And, of course, there was a large crowd gathering and lots of people offering advice on how to fix the vehicles; who should back up, whose fault it was and so on. We stopped for a truck lunch and to see whether a tow truck would arrive to get the road clear.

As we ate, it became obvious that there was an alternative route, and Gareth stopped and talked to enough other lorry drivers to work out a suitable route for us. It was being used by some lorries without loads and the ground was uneven. It sloped steeply, so it was not passable by the more heavily laden trucks, which had to queue up on the road, waiting for the blockage to be cleared, but lighter empty trucks were able to get through.

And, of course, this was Africa where just about all the lorries are overloaded; and most of the cars were also overloaded, with perhaps six or eight people inside, and a huge load strapped to the roof, doubling the height of the car, plus perhaps a couple of people lying on top of the bags on the roof. They also bounced across the rough ground, with both drivers and passengers determined not to be delayed by a broken-down lorry.

We took the unofficial diversion and moved on towards Conakry. The original settlement was on the island which Great Britain ceded to France in 1887, and it became the capital of Guinea in 1904. The city has now expanded along the peninsula, and its population is now about two million, which is a sixth of the country's total population.

It was getting late in the afternoon and we were some sixty kilometres short of the border, so we turned off, to find a bush camp. Kim stopped, and walked up a track, and returned with a crowd of more than twenty children, mostly boys and a few adults. The track went to a soccer field where they had been playing a game, and amongst the adults was the headman of the village.

Therefore, we negotiated with him, and we could camp on their football field. After some of the rough ground that we had camped on, this was a lovely flat area; sandy, level and soft. We were watched until a long time after sunset, as we set up camp. We lit the fire and put the tents up, watched by a score of children, sitting quietly on the ground, as if we were the best thing since sliced bread, or as if they were watching a film. Some of the girls left to do chores at home.

Later, after a couple of hours, they started to say goodnight and got up to leave. The crowd thinned. We thanked the headman and donated some food to the village, in return for letting us use their playing field. There was a small group left and some remained and were joined by other villagers, mostly women and daughters who had finished their chores and had come to see the white travellers.

There was not much to see, as half of the group had gone to bed. The kitchen was packed away, and the fire was just embers, glowing red in the dark. We were eventually left in relative peace, except for a few youngsters on motorbikes at the far end of the football field who had music playing on their phones with the volume turned right up, so that the sound quality was poor which made sleeping difficult. In the morning, the headman came to check on us to ensure that everything was all right. He seemed content that he had helped some travellers and that we were satisfied with his hospitality.

CHAPTER 8
SIERRA LEONE

We drove on to the border which was only seventy kilometres away, but it took more than two and a half hours to get there, over poor roads. Getting out of a country is usually easy, and we had already obtained our visas, but it still took more than two hours to get through the border.

We paid our road toll at the Pamelap toll booth. And it was there that I noticed a change in the traffic. Several of the cars were bright, new, shiny and cared for. They didn't have dents, they weren't rusty, and the engines seemed to run smoothly. It is interesting what you can get used to, but only when I commented on it, did other people also agree. Not only that but there were also no the cars with eight people inside and another couple on the roof, with the usual stack of bags, bundles, furniture, animals and other paraphernalia.

The small village of Pamelap is dominated by the hotel. It lurks on the roundabout and is the tallest building around. The old building is a three storey, decayed concrete structure with empty windows, blackened walls from mildew, and grass growing out of every crack and across the top of the building. It sits sideways on to the roundabout with a view down the main road. The rooms on the opposite side of the building to the roundabout are overlooking a stunning view, as the hillside plunges down into the valley. It is a great location, but is not an operational hotel.

There is another building under construction and possibly taller. It sits with its long elevation facing across the roundabout, and down the road towards Freetown. It is so large that it can only be a future hotel, but it might be another season before it is completed and operational.

And then it was just a short drive over relatively good roads, through a mix of open savannah with a few palms and grasses in between, to get to Waterloo, on the outskirts of the urban fringe that surrounds Freetown. You know when you are getting closer to any major city centre, as there are suddenly more building sites; the buildings are larger and have more storeys, and there is more plastic rubbish blowing about. The traffic increases, there are even more people, if that is possible in an African town, and there are a greater number and variety of shops and stalls along the roadside. We headed to the south western coast of the peninsula to find our beach camp at Bureh Beach Surf Club. It was set up as a community project by a European surfer, more than a decade ago.

Freetown is the capital of Sierra Leone, and the country gained independence in 1961. English is the official language. The two largest ethnic groups are the Temne, found predominantly in the north of the country, and the Mende in the south east, each with its own customs and languages. There is also a small group of Krio who are descended from freed African American and West Indian slaves. They speak an English based creole, which unites the country, as it is spoken by ninety-seven percent of the population.

The initial population of Krios comprised freed slaves from the American War of Independence. When British troops left America, they also evacuated many liberated slaves, and escaped slaves, who had helped the British forces. They were originally evacuated to London but were subsequently relocated to Sierra Leone. Nearly five hundred settlers arrived in 1787.

There was another group of three thousand Black Loyalists, who had been relocated and granted land in Nova Scotia. They founded Birchtown in Nova Scotia, which still exists today, and the town boasts the Black Loyalists Heritage Centre, just fifty metres from the town's museum. They faced harsh winters and discrimination from white settlers, in nearby Shelburne. A group of twelve hundred of these Black Loyalists were relocated to Freetown in 1792.

The existing Krio population had another boost in the year 1800, when British naval vessels relocated five hundred Jamaican Maroons. Maroons was a generic term for former slaves who had escaped slavery and had set up their own communities in remote inland areas of the Caribbean, and some South American colonies. They were a constant source of tension, as they occasionally raided plantations to liberate other slaves, and to collect supplies. They, in turn, were subject to raids by settlers to re-enslave them. Their existence also made expansion of plantations into the interior a risky enterprise. Therefore, some of them were offered the opportunity to relocate and to establish legitimate communities.

The Krio population was constantly increased by the British navy. Britain had made the slave trade illegal in 1807 and abolished slavery in 1833. When a British naval ship intercepted a slave ship, the slaves would be liberated and taken to Freetown. Many settled in the town, but there were abuses, as some were still treated as slaves and second-class citizens. Some found life in Freetown intolerable, and settled in the interior. Some even walked through the jungle, hundreds of kilometres back to their original village.

The country has a significant mining sector. There are extensive reserves of rutile (the ore from which titanium is produced), bauxite, diamonds and gold. But despite this potential wealth, over seventy percent of the population live in poverty.

The Portuguese explorer, Pedro de Sintra discovered and mapped the hills behind the large harbour in Freetown in 1462. It is considered the third largest natural harbour in the world. He called the mountains Serra Leoa – Lioness Mountain. Over time, the area became known as Sierra Leone.

English and French traders also set up trade here. In 1562, Sir John Hawkins of the English navy bought three hundred slaves here, and transported them to Santo Domingo or Hispaniola, in the Caribbean, thus initiating the Triangle Trade. This was used for transporting trade goods to Africa, to buy slaves and gold and then to transport them to the Americas and the Caribbean, and then to trade the slaves for sugar, rum, tobacco and cotton to take back to Europe.

We had booked a taxi for nine a.m. to take us into Freetown, and it hadn't arrived. I wasn't in the best of moods anyway, as I had had a bad night. There was an election the night before and the hotel along the beach had hosted a candidate's election party for a local headman, and he had won with a majority of three hundred and fifty votes, so there was loud music all night. I was awake for most of the night, because of the noise from the party next door, and the noise from the night owls in our group, who sat up talking and drinking just inches from my tent. I was closer to some of the owls than they were to their compatriots on the other side of the table. It was my fault for pitching my tent there, but there weren't many other places to pitch a tent.

I went for a three kilometre walk to the junction with the main road. I was filling in time and hoping that the owls would move to the beach or to the truck. I came across another party at the junction with the main road. There was a gas station and a police checkpoint so I felt reasonably safe. There was loud music, dancing and loads of people hanging out. The noise and the people had initially put me off going any closer, but I was intrigued, and I summoned up the courage to go from the dark into the bright lights and the centre of the party.

It wasn't an event, but just a place for people to meet up and hang out. The garage sold cold soft drinks and snacks. There were lots of car horns honking, the high-pitched whine of moped horns, shouting of hellos and goodbyes as people came or went, plus a few bottles of drink in brown paper bags being passed around.

I walked home alone in the dark, and despite the late hour, the owls were still awake, chatting and drinking. I walked along the beach several times in both directions. The owls moved down to a fire on the beach sometime after midnight, and I went to my tent.

One of the beach club staff had to get the taxi driver out of bed. It took some persistence and negotiating as the price had changed from USD30 for the round trip to USD30 per person. We all got out and after some hard bargaining, two people still didn't want to go, but seven of us took the taxi into town. There was congestion and the one-hour journey overran by an hour.

We got out near the Cotton Tree and spilt up. The Cotton Tree is a giant and ancient tree and an iconic image of Freetown, which stands out above the rooftops of the city. There are reports that freed slaves sheltered from the sun, under the tree, and it is known that it existed in 1787, which makes it well over two hundred years old, and that some Black Loyalists from Nova Scotia prayed under it in 1792. I visited the National Museum en route to the internet café. There was no internet at the beachfront and I needed access to Wi-Fi and email. I also wanted a break from camping, so I was looking for a hotel.

Whilst walking about Freetown, I came across a lovely turn of the century building down by the docks, with the date 1898 at the apex underneath the roof. It was painted black, with windows and doors picked out in red. It advertised vodka and Jodee's Relaxation. It was open in the evening, and late into the night as a drinking den, and probably a brothel. It was daytime, but the door was open, so I went in as I was inquisitive. There were some girls doing chores around the place, but the eldest woman came over to greet me. She had worked here for decades and in her words, she was an entrepreneur and a proprietor, introducing herself as Mrs Quee, and we spent some time chatting. She directed me to a good hotel up the road, The International which was within my price range but, on arrival, I checked and there was no internet.

I went to my first option on Aberdeen, at the north end of a peninsula on top of a rocky outcrop, which catches any breeze. It is the best location in the city but not the cheapest by a long way. I caught a tuk tuk from near the Cotton Tree. I flagged one down at random, but he was not going to take me there. It was too far and there would be no return fare. I pressed him, then he quoted an exorbitant fare. I negotiated and settled for something that I thought was reasonable. His name was George, and he wanted to emigrate to England. He was also a chorister at the local church, and he sang several hymns as he drove the tuk tuk over potholes, to get me to my hotel.

One of the major tourist attractions in the city that I wanted to visit, was the National Railway Museum. It is only open by special appointment on a Saturday. It is shut on Sundays and as I was visiting over the New Year holidays, it was shut for a bank holiday on Monday, so I never got to see it.

    I didn't want to use my credit card more than possible, so I needed to get to an ATM. I checked at reception but there were none within walking distance, so I had to take a taxi. I walked to the front of the queue of taxis outside the hotel and was driven to several ATM's before we found one that worked, which was just about at the same place that I had been in, earlier in the day. I drew out as much as I could, and then I spent half of what I got out to pay for the taxi, and so I was still short of cash.

    The Bintumani Hotel sits in a great position on the top of a hill, on an island with marine views on three sides and, on the fourth side, a view of the causeway and the road connection to the top end of the peninsula, on which Freetown is built. I had read about the hotel years before, and it was a classic building of the colonial period. However, it has since been redeveloped, using Chinese money, into a large five-storey concrete block, with signs everywhere in Chinese, Chinese guests and of course, Chinese food for the breakfast buffet and evening meal, although there was a limited Western selection. It wasn't quite the colonial atmosphere that I had hoped for, but it had a selection of marvellous local fish dishes in the restaurant.

    At the end of my stay, I paid my bill and went to the taxi rank. I was quoted an outrageous price, so I had to negotiate. I got the quote down to about half of what I had been quoted initially, and near enough to what I had paid to get into Freetown a few days earlier. Then the driver threw a wobbly and said that for journeys outside the city, the passenger had to pay for the petrol, adding that it was customary. True or false? Had I bargained too hard and this was his way of getting a little back? I have no idea, but we weren't getting anywhere, so I had to fork out for petrol but at least it was cheap.

    He was taking me to York village, a little guest house fifteen kilometres from where I would be meeting the others and Nala at the beach the next morning. The taxis and its timing are unreliable so I wanted to be close enough to give myself a lot of slack so I wouldn't miss the departure. The taxi driver was chatty and interesting. His name was Brian, and this was another first as I have never met any African called Brian. He was full of interesting anecdotes, history, local knowledge and the like, and must have chatted for most of the journey.

There were a lot of posters for the forthcoming elections in two months. Politics is always a difficult topic to speak about when you are not sure of a person's political views, but I went ahead anyway. Brian was adamant that Samura Kamara was not only the best candidate, but also that he had a strong following and would be the winner. As it happened, his major opponent, Julius Maada Bio was elected as president a few weeks later on the second round of voting, with a majority of just 51.8 percent of the vote, a majority of about fifteen thousand votes.

York is halfway down the west side of the peninsula, but because the roads on the west side are so bad, it is faster to drive down the length of the peninsula on the east side, and then drive back up the west side, three times the distance.

To get back to the Bureh Beach Surf Club, I had ordered my taxi the night before, and as predicted six a.m. came and went, and there was no sign of a taxi, not even the distant rumble of an engine to disturb the morning peace.

I went around knocking on doors until I found someone, and I explained that I had ordered a taxi and it wasn't here. There was a lot of phoning and shouting down the phone and eventually, a taxi turned up. He didn't greet me, he just said a hundred thousand. It was far too much, and I countered with thirty thousand. After some negotiation we settled on fifty thousand which was about the same cost per kilometre as the other taxi rides.

I thought that the taxi ride ought to take about twenty minutes, but my driver did the journey in less than ten minutes. He took the racing line on every corner, relying on the fact that it was dark, and that there were no other headlights on the road, but ignoring other potential obstacles such as bicycles without lights and pedestrians.

I arrived at the Bureh Beach Surf Club without mishap, other than for a few bruises where I had been thrown sideways on some particularly tight bends. I had missed breakfast, but at least I had not missed the departure time. But there was one less person as Noah had left the group to do his own thing, and although he said he would meet up with us soon, we never saw him again.

We drove all day back the way we had come, via Waterloo and on to Makeni where we stopped to do a cook group shop. We were used to markets where all the food stalls were close together. Here it was different, and the food was mixed in with the general merchandise. It was hard to find some things. We looked for beef but saw none but found a shop that had frozen food with some nice-looking frozen chicken. We would be having Hungarian goulash using chicken instead of beef.

Vegetables were also difficult. Onions were easy, but we found no tomatoes. We found a vegetable that looked like a tomato, red and round but firmer, but they turned out to be very bitter. We found some expensive potatoes and loose, dried butter beans, and we exhausted the budget. We didn't have enough, so I chipped in from my own pocket, but at least the meat eaters would have a chicken leg each. It was late in the afternoon when we left Makeni but there was a memorable sight of large fruit bats flying about above the town, as we left.

We drove north east from Makeni and the road was adequate and there was little traffic on it. The tarmac ended, and we were travelling along a dirt track. Road improvements had been started. There were some new culverts and bridges over the larger streams, but there were many unfinished bridges and embankments. The road in places was just sand and in other places it was gravel, but unfinished. A road improvement project had been started but never finished.

There was an outbreak of Ebola in Guinea in December 2013. Ebola is a viral haemorrhagic fever and initial symptoms are fever, sore throat, muscular pain and headaches. Then patients start vomiting and suffer from diarrhoea, a rash and decreased liver and kidney function, with internal and external bleeding. Untreated, the mortality rate is over seventy percent and even in hospitalised cases, mortality is nearly sixty percent. Cases were reported later in Sierra Leone and Liberia.

It was devastating for individuals and their families, but it also caused widespread social and economic hardship. The number of cases peaked in October 2014, and then gradually declined. There were over twenty-eight thousand cases and eleven thousand deaths. Many of the survivors suffer from post Ebola syndrome, requiring ongoing medical care. The disease can remain dormant and may return months later. A major international relief effort followed, to contain the outbreak, but it also caused havoc to local government budgets, and it put a lot of strain on local medical facilities. As medical staff around the world gave assistance, many expatriate workers left, and development projects were shelved. Hence, the partially constructed road and the lack of any ongoing work. The last case was recorded in Liberia in June 2016, but there was another outbreak in the Democratic Republic of the Congo, in 2018.

There were partly built culverts with shuttering to hold the concrete where the track dipped to one side, to go around an unfinished obstacle. Further on, there were no more signs of any building work. It was just the old deeply rutted track. It was bumpy and slow going. The overhanging trees showered us with leaves, twigs and insects as we brushed past.

It took two days to get near the border. We camped in a quarry just sixty-four kilometres short of the border, but it took us another eight hours of driving. We crossed the Sierra Leone border and stopped in a small village. It was getting late and the Guinea border which was another six kilometres away would be closed. We found the village headman, and he agreed that we could camp on the village football pitch for the night, our second bush camp on a football pitch.

CHAPTER 9
GUINEA CONAKRY AGAIN

We set out for the border and went through customs first, and they stamped our passports. Then we drove up the road and stopped at immigration and then there was a problem, as the customs had stamped our passports, and the captain on duty made a big scene. He claimed it was extra work and so he couldn't let us through; a clear hint in Africa for a bribe.

Several people came through the office, handed over some money, got a stamp and carried on, as if it was a locally well-known scam between the customs and the immigration officials. Perhaps we should just have slipped him a few notes, but we don't bribe on principle. By perpetuating the practice, we would make it harder for other travellers, so we stand our ground. After making a big fuss, we could go on our way, but we had to stop at the next town at Faranah, and report to the immigration office to give an explanation, have our stamps sorted out and to obtain the correct paperwork to show to the next official.

In Faranah, while Kim was talking to the immigration officials with all our passports, I tried to find a post office and I asked several people who directed me to several buildings. I ended up outside the police station, the local radio station, the immigration office and under the tall telecommunications tower on top of the hill. One official asked me why I was in his office, I had been directed there. He escorted me outside, and he pointed to another building down the road, which was the police station which I had already visited. Everyone wanted to be helpful, but I didn't find the post office.

Then on again to Kissidougou. En route, we passed several wildfires. The savannah was tinder dry after a long dry season. The rainy season would start any day, but until it did, there would be wildfires. The first one you see is memorable. There was a bush burning at the side of road. There was crackling as the fire consumed the bush, and there was searing heat as we passed. Flames leapt into the air and there was a heat haze and embers floating up into the sky above the bush, only to fall back again and start another wildfire.

Throughout the savannah there were paths, but it is odd to see how sometimes everything is burnt but the dry grass that had been trampled on the path doesn't catch fire. There was black ash either side of the path, with dried grass marking the route, as it snaked around trees and the charred remains of bushes. The fire couldn't cross a road as it formed a firebreak but I did wonder why the fire would stop in one place but carry on elsewhere. Blackened remains might stretch right up to dense grass and shrubs which were untouched and escaped bring destroyed. Looking out across the savannah, you could see plumes of grey smoke rising from other fires.

Nobody does anything about them. Most of the fields had been harvested long before or the plants were not close enough to continue spreading the fire. Some houses had hard packed earth around them, leaving nothing to burn. The only time that anybody seemed to be doing anything regarding fires was to encourage them to burn through shrubs to clear the land for planting.

We found a bush camp on the far side of Kissidougou in a former quarry. There was also a former lumber cutting area. There were offcuts and oddly shaped pieces left behind. We helped ourselves and replenished the wood locker.

In mid-afternoon the road crossed a river and there were palabas for shade on the river bank. It was a local picnic site and swimming hole. We stopped for an hour for a swim. We had been bush camping for a while, and our feet were still black from the ash from fires, so it was also an opportunity to have a good soak.

It was another long drive day to ultimately reach another camp down by the Guinea – Cote d'Ivorie border, in a remote area. We stopped at the bustling city of Lola. We stopped near the market which was colourful, noisy and characterful. There was also a hospital nearby and we filled our jerry cans from their taps. It was also an opportunity for me to check out the hospital. It was well-planned and the different departments were well signposted and the staff were in uniforms. I didn't experience how well they delivered their services but it seemed to function, and I was surprised at how efficient it looked as I hadn't been sure what to expect, but it was so much better than I had envisioned, and it was facilities like this that were the front line in the most recent Ebola crisis.

The road from there to the border was being upgraded, but unlike many of the other projects we had passed, this one had workers and machinery and they were building the road. There were workers everywhere and big yellow digging machines, graders, levellers and tarmac machines, being operated by locals but the people in charge were all Chinese, and all the equipment was Chinese.

The old road was being straightened and gentle curves and gradients created through cuttings or over embankments. Meanwhile, the old road twisted through jungle and crossed the earthworks to weave its way through jungle on the other side of the building site. We reached a junction with signs denoting the way to Côte d'Ivoire and to Liberia. If I was going to stick to my original plan to follow the coast down the western side of Africa, I should have planned on visiting Liberia.

Liberia is unusual in Africa, as it was not a colony of a European power as it was colonised by the American Colonisation Society, which was established in 1816. They believed that African Americans had a better chance of living their own lives if they were repatriated to Africa. Its supporters came from all levels of society as did its opponents. Evangelists and Quakers were often anti-slavery and truly thought that it would make their lives better. Slave holders and supporters believed that they could remove freed slaves and free-born blacks from their society. Others believed the society to be racist, as some of the former slaves wanted to remain in the country of their birth, and to promote equal rights within America.

Either way, between 1816 and 1861, the society repatriated fifteen thousand African Americans and three thousand Afro Caribbean's to Liberia, also known as the Pepper Coast. Liberia declared independence in 1842 and was the first African state to declare independence as a modern republic. America did not recognise the new country until 1862. It suffered in the late twentieth century from two civil wars between 1989 and 2003 with just a brief two-year period of peace. More than a quarter of a million people died, about eight percent of the population; and the economy shrunk by ninety percent. Stability was threatened again with the outbreak of Ebola.

Illegal logging has been a problem, leading to deforestation. There is a lot of bush meat eaten there, including endangered species. A survey showed that thirteen percent of households eat bush meat once a week and seven percent cook bush meat every day. It may be safe to visit the capital, Monrovia with precautions, but the country is considered dangerous, and I avoided it.

We turned off the road at Bossou, which hosts a centre for chimpanzee observation, a research centre and although open to the public, it's so remote that there aren't many visitors but, due to the remoteness and the lack of visitors, it is a favoured location to carry out chimpanzee research.

We left the main road and went straight on into the jungle, along a narrow track. We came to a bridge that looked as if it had suffered some damage and there were holes in the roadbed. Gareth got out and checked the bridge before crossing. Up the slope on the far side was a broken-down lorry, blocking the track. Motorbikes could squeeze past but there was no space for cars or trucks, so we pulled over to one side and stopped.

The truck had broken down in gear, so the driver was removing the crank shaft. Then it rolled back down the slope and wedged itself against a tree. With a lot of pushing it was disentangled from the tree and gently and under control, it rolled back to the bottom of the slope and came to a halt at the side of the road and there was enough space for us to continue.

We stopped at the Institute de recherche d'environmental de Bossou and set up camp in their grounds. They offer treks into the forest to see the chimpanzees, which leaves at eight a.m. The animals can be mischievous, so it is best not to take too much stuff with you, and to always hold on to your camera.

From Bossou it was just forty-four kilometres to lunch, but it took us four hours. It was slow progress as the temporary road had a poor surface and wound through the jungle and criss crossed the new but unopened smooth road surface. One section was left unmolested by the builders; a long section of flat land covered in stands of bamboo, which towered over us, but gave us shade from the burning sun. Then we re-joined the road builders, and the chaos of their building site to cross the border into Côte d'Ivoire.

CHAPTER 10
CÔTE D'IVOIRE

We had obtained visas in Rabat in Morocco several weeks before, so it was merely formalities to be stamped out of Guinea, then a hundred metre drive further to reach the Côte d'Ivoire border crossing. We were through without any problem, but the truck took another half an hour. However, the extra time gave us an opportunity to change money with the local money changer. There were signs everywhere about Ebola and there were hand sanitisers and signs telling you to wash your hands.

Then it was another hour's drive to get to the customs. They knew we were coming, and they had stayed open, waiting for us to arrive. It was dusk when we cleared customs, and it would be difficult to find a bush camp in the dark. The customs officials seemed like nice people, so we asked them whether we could camp in their grounds, and they were happy to let us do that.

I was part of the cook group again, but with a small group the chores seemed to come around often. We had lit the fire and were chopping vegetables. To my shame, I had lost the key to the truck. When not in use, the key is on a lanyard, so it can hang around your neck, so it can't fall out of your pocket or get lost. Somehow, I had lost it. I continued cooking while some of the others searched the ground and rummaged through my things. Someone found it, and I can't explain how it happened and I didn't notice but I had put my tent up before starting cooking. The key on its lanyard had become stuck to some Velcro on the tent. It was an embarrassing moment but with a happy outcome.

Côte d'Ivoire became a French protectorate in 1843, and a colony in 1893. It became independent in 1960, and was ruled by its president, Félix Houphouët-Boigny until 1993. The country's name has often been translated into other languages, and this had caused a problem with the government, in its international dealings. Therefore, in April 1986, the government declared that the country's formal name would henceforth be Côte d'Ivoire, for purposes of diplomatic protocol and it refused to recognise any other form. That is also the reason why I have used Côte d'Ivoire, rather than the Ivory Coast, as a sop to my hosts. The country's wealth is built upon coffee, cocoa, timber, oil, palm oil, rubber and pineapples. Cocoa makes up forty percent of their exports, followed by oil and oil products at twenty percent. Ivory used to make a major contribution until most of the elephants were killed.

There were several long driving days as we crossed the country. After Guezon, we crossed the Sassandra River which flows into Lac de Buyo. This reservoir was created in 1980, when the river had a dam built across it to provide hydroelectric power and the power house can generate 165MW of electricity.

After passing through Daloa, it was getting late, and we turned up a track disappearing into a rubber plantation. As we went down the track the branches over hung the track, and we were being covered in leaves and dust, as we brushed past. Then Noodles jumped up and started banging the seat and swearing. We had upset a nest of tree ants which had been knocked into the truck. They had large pincers and were naturally protecting their larvae and were biting her with a vengeance. She is a vegetarian and shows a lot of respect to wildlife, however small, ugly or dangerous, so this was quite out of character. We all joined in, getting rid of the ants and the larvae, and we were more cautious, stooping low and away from the windows as the truck continued into the plantation.

As it happened it was an ideal bush campsite, set well back from the road, with no nearby buildings, a flat area and plenty of firewood from the thinning from the plantation. We were deep in a rubber plantation, and even though we were out of town and it was dark, there were still people about. A chap with a machete came past and stopped to watch us. He was joined by a couple of other men walking back from work, and later a couple of motor bikes came past and stopped. In Africa, there is always someone nearby, so be warned! It may seem empty but there are always people about, to see what's happening.

I had gone to answer a call of nature and thought that I was far enough from the track, not to be disturbed for a few moments. I was just about to stop, when I heard voices and two people were walking towards me. I acted nonchalantly and walked on, greeting them in French with a cheery good evening and I waited until there was enough distance between us, before dipping into the trees.

It was a warm night, and I slept on top of my inflatable mattress as it was so warm and humid. During the night, several of us heard a large animal walk through the camp, but no one was quick enough with a torch, to look outside and see what it was. Speculation was rife about what it was; including lions, leopards and elephants, and just about any other big animal indigenous to Africa. It would get into everybody's tales of the trip as a huge wild beast, but it was probably just a lost goat.

The workers were back early in the morning, and they were watching us from a distance, as we cooked breakfast and took our tents down. Eventually, some of them were brave enough to come over and speak to us, and we exchanged greetings in French. They had brought some coconuts, which we exchanged for some honey and a pineapple.

We stopped at Yamoussoukro to see the Basilica of Our Lady of the Peace. It is modelled upon but is not a copy of the Basilica of Saint Peter in Rome. It is a vast modern church, that, according to the Guinness book of records, is the largest church in the world that sits on a low hill next to a river. Construction started in 1985 and was completed in 1990. Its cost allegedly ranges from USD175 per metre, to USD600 per metre, and attracted a lot of criticism for the outlandish cost of a self-ingratiating project, that sucked up vital government resources.

Yamoussoukro was the birth place of president Félix Houphouët-Boigny. He was one of the classic Big Man dictators in Africa.

He spent huge sums on an expensive and vain project to glorify himself, with six lane highways leading to nowhere, and he arbitrarily moved the capital from Abidjan to Yamoussoukro in 1983. Abidjan remains the administrative centre and most countries maintain an embassy in Abidjan. The church is a huge building covering thirty thousand square metres and stands a hundred and fifty-eight metres high. There are some beautiful stained-glass windows but it does seem to be an extravagant use of money when there are so many other pressing needs for such a developing country.

It was a sticky hot and humid drive over two hundred and thirty kilometres down the main road to Abidjan, and through it to a beach resort near Grand-Bassam. Abidjan was a great place. It was the first modern business centre that we had seen for weeks, since leaving Morocco. There were supermarkets, bars, cinemas, high rise buildings, motorways, flyovers and all sorts of things that many of us take for granted in a city that we hadn't seen for weeks. But we weren't stopping. We were just passing through it to find our beachfront camp site.

We found the Bla-Siweka Hotel and beach resort, and we parked in the grounds, and set up our tents. I had a quick but hot shower and I then moved on to the bar and I ordered my favourite, fish and more specifically, barracuda which has a solid, white fleshed meat.

The next morning I boarded a kombi, a minibus that follows a scheduled route into Grand-Bassam to get a phone, a SIM card and a battery power pack. I also wanted a universal battery recharger, but I was out of luck with that, but at least I now had a phone that connected to the local network.

The next morning it rained. What is so special about rain that it gets a mention? I hadn't seen any rain for weeks since Agadir and crossing vast stretches of desert and savannah. Rain in Africa is different. It comes down in fast torrents, large rain drops that beat on the roofs and pound the leaves of the palm trees. The noise was substantial, but just as suddenly as it started, it stopped, and the clouds blew over, and it was just another ordinary day.

I didn't look carefully at the destination board, under the windscreen of the kombi that I had taken. It wasn't going to Grand-Bassam, but it took the bypass and was going over the bridge, over the river on to Bonoua. The driver and the conductor didn't speak French, but some local language that I didn't understand, but it was clear that he was telling me to get out, in a polite manner as he knew that I was on the wrong kombi, and he pointed me back into the town centre.

After walking around the centre of Grand-Bassam, I had a long walk to get back to my hotel, but I walked along the edge of the main road and I hoped to flag down a kombi going my way. It was only when I got back to the junction between the main road and the bypass, that I was able to flag down a kombi to get back to the campsite.

CHAPTER 11
GHANA

It was a noisy night, as the wind rustled the palm fronds., which sounded like rain, but it was dry and airless at ground level. It was hot and sticky in the tent. There was a breeze at a height, but nothing moved near the ground.

I was up early for the departure, to drive back through Abidjan, to drive north on some good roads, to get to the border to cross from Côte d'Ivoire into Ghana. It was one of the few times that we not only had to show our passports, but we also had to show our yellow fever immunisation cards at the border. We also had our temperatures taken, to ensure that we weren't suffering from any fever.

In Ghana I noticed another change in the people and the culture, especially the language. For the first time in some months since leaving The Gambia we were in a country where English is the main language. We stopped in Sanyani for shopping, and again at the Kintampo Falls.

This is the largest series of waterfalls in Ghana. It starts with two waterfalls that fall for twenty-five metres, and then crosses some rocks and at one point the river disappears under some boulders. That section is followed by another waterfall with a seventy metre drop. There is a long stairway to negotiate to get to the bottom, but it is worth the effort. At the bottom of the waterfall it is only knee deep, but it was another opportunity for a splash. It was not deep enough to swim but it was an opportunity to have a good soak to get rid of some of the ingrained dirt from days and days of bush camping.

It took another couple of days to reach the Mole National Park in the north of the country. There are dusk and dawn safari walks to see animals and the big one to see here are the elephants. There was a sign showing many of the animals that you might see, and I was happy to see elephants, but I wanted to see the pangolin, a scaly ant eater, but I would be lucky to see them as they are timid animals, and nocturnal and if threatened they roll themselves up into a ball like a hedgehog.

As soon as we arrived, I booked an evening trek. I was at the main centre to meet my guide, Sadique, armed with a Lee Enfield 0.303 rifle, so battered and worn that it was probably left over from the First World War. He gave us a brief talk on safety in the jungle and then we set off into the trees.

We saw and tracked two juvenile elephants as they foraged in the trees for something to eat. We crept forward and then they would move on. We followed and sometimes they would turn to face us and wiggle their ears and snort. Then they would turn and walk off into some thicker shrub to conceal themselves. We would follow but after an hour, we left them to try and find something else to see.

We had been warned about honey badgers. It is not actually a badger but more closely related to a weasel. It is a carnivore. It has few natural predators and a well-deserved reputation for its aggressive attitude and especially for defending itself. If you see one you need to back off, as it can be unpredictably vicious with sharp teeth and claws.

There was also meant to be antelope and we saw a few specimens, but they rarely stayed still enough for a good photo before disappearing into the bush. We walked through the savannah for a long time before returning to the campsite. There was a still haze over the countryside from the dust and the smoke from bush fires.

It was a short night as I was up again for a dawn safari, with another armed guide and a friend of Sadique named Majid. We hadn't gone a hundred metres from the centre when we came across three juvenile elephants. We took photos and tracked them for a while, until we all had enough photos and were ready to go and find something else. We found more antelope, loads of birds, including the grey headed kingfisher, ibis, palm nut vultures and many, many more.

Majid pointed out several trees with medicinal purposes; one that relieved asthma, another which eased hernias, another that was a general pick me up, and yet another which aided the digestion and relieved stomach aches. There was a place where there were naturally occurring salt licks for animals and the animals would also seek out certain plants that had medicinal uses for them. The forest is a medicine cabinet if you know enough about it. Many modern medicines are based on the natural compounds found in plants, used by the indigenous peoples.

The next large town that we stopped in was Kumasi. This is the traditional capital of the Ashanti nation. It has the largest open market in West Africa. It was my first introduction to a fetish market, a place where you can find anything from leopard heads and human skulls to priests who can create fetishes, predict the future and make medicines to heal whatever might afflict you. Voodoo is often associated with Haiti in the Caribbean, but it was only taken there by slaves from Africa, where its origins can be found. There were a series of stalls selling whole dried animals and parts of animals, heads, skulls, skins, bones and shrivelled, unrecognisable parts of animals. There were even parts of some endangered species, but the folklore only meant that rarity meant greater power, and of course more expensive. There were several stalls, so it seemed that there was enough custom for the stallholders to make a living.

This area is a major hardwood, cocoa and coffee producing area, but is also home to AngloGold Ashanti, which has several mines in the vicinity and is one of the world's largest gold producers. The country was previously known as the Gold Coast due to the large amounts of gold that it produced, traditionally, for centuries. There are several mines in the country, but gold mining has moved on from historical artisanal producers and now, there are big mining companies involved, with massive investments in plants, mines and ore processing plants. In 2016 the country produced ninety tons of gold, the second largest producer in Africa, after South Africa, which produced a hundred and forty tons a year. But it is only ranked as the eleventh largest producer in the world, and it is a long way behind the largest, such as the top three producers, namely, China at four hundred and fifty-five tons, Australia at two hundred and seventy tons and Russia at two hundred and fifty tons.

We had a bush camp planned down a long track, close to a cocoa plantation. But we had to obtain permission from the boss man, and it took a while, during which time the sun had set, and we would not be able to find another campsite. However, the man in charge was very hospitable and he allowed us to stay on his front lawn. He introduced himself as Mr Charles. He was the manager of the governmental Seed Protection Division.

Their role is to produce cocoa seeds and to grow trees, which are then given to the local farmers to grow a high-quality cocoa crop. We walked into town and we found the Roof Top Bar. It was shut but the bar underneath was open, the Roof Down Bar, a smaller road frontage version of the same operation. The roof top bar is open at weekends and on special occasions.

It was one of the noisiest camps that we had ever stayed at. There was noise coming from the bars along the main road until early into the morning. There was noise from the constant passage of heavy trucks, motorbikes and people shouting. The music in the bars flowed out across the road and into the surrounding jungle.

I managed to get some sleep, despite the noise, but I was awake again at four a.m. There was some gospel singing going on next door. There were crickets and other insects buzzing or clicking away, and the noise of the forest at night. The cockerels were crowing. There were choirs singing to the accompaniment of organs, drums and pianos. The muezzins were calling the faithful to prayer. There was music pouring out of the cafés that had opened early. Someone started to ring a bell, but it wasn't a clear tone, it was slightly off key, and it had a crack in it, giving it a peculiar sound that ground on the nerves.

The only thing that I expected to hear and didn't, was dogs barking, but surprisingly, there weren't any. Also, the birds including a colony of crows nesting in the trees around us were silent until the sun started to lighten the sky, and only then did they add their calls to the cacophony.

Mr Charles took us on a tour of the research station, and he explained the various processes required to produce what we know as chocolate. The cocoa pods are yellow, the shape of a rugby ball, but two thirds of the size, with white seeds inside. The seeds and the pith are removed and left in a locker to ferment for six days. They are then removed; the surplus pith is removed, and the seeds are placed in a drier. This particular one was a row of planks between two walls, which allowed air to circulate. Then the seeds are sold to commercial enterprises who then process the seeds to obtain the chocolate that they want.

The research centre grows trees from seeds which are planted and nurtured and then when they are between one month and six months old, the plants are given to local farmers. Those trees will start producing a crop after three years and will last for thirty-five years. Hybrids are grown locally, but the Amazonia's type is popular with international cocoa buyers and it is largely exported. Ghana produces some of the best quality cocoa beans in the world, and some of that is due to government support and research stations like this one, of which there are several in the cocoa growing regions.

The station has several fields of coca, but they also grow other plants such as mangos and plantains. These are planted with the cocoa trees, to provide shade for the young cocoa plants until they have become established. Even the husks are used. They are broken down and either left to decompose into compost to be used as fertiliser or they can be made into a simple form of soap for local usage.

We were staying at the Presbyterian Mission not far from the central market which it is claimed to be the largest in West Africa with over eleven thousand stalls and it was certainly large, heaving with people, noisy and colourful. We camped on a patch of grass opposite the main building within a walled complex not far from the main Presbyterian church. Inside were showers with hot water and clean toilets. There were also spare rooms and so some of the group upgraded to a bed there.

That evening we took a taxi to go to the View, a highly recommended restaurant, but the driver didn't know about it and it didn't appear on our maps or on our phones. We were on the right road and rather than run up a large taxi fare as he stopped and asked for directions, we got out and walked. We asked repeatedly for directions and those who knew the restaurant were consistent by pointing down the road. It was dark by the time we got there, and two kilometres from where we had got out of the taxi, but it was worth the effort as the food was good, although it wasn't cheap.

After a few days to recuperate, we drove towards the coast and stopped en route to visit the Kakum National Park. It was established as a reserve in 1931, but only became a national park in 1992. The entry price seemed expensive and it would close in two hours so we only took a quick walk along some of the paths. It is famous as it is one of only three parks in Africa that has an elevated walkway, which goes through the treetop jungle canopy for three hundred and fifty metres. After Mole where we had seen elephants, this seemed a bit of a disappointment, as there were no large animals to see. Then it was a short drive to Elmina on the coast for a camp on the beach at the Stumble Inn.

I walked along the beach from the beach camp to Elmina. Outside the town, there is a fishing village, and as I walked through it, I passed a lot of fish drying in the sun. In the castle I meet my local guide, Felix who guided me around the town. We saw the Saint Georges Fort, which sits at the mouth of the river and inland, the Saint Joseph's fort. The Portuguese first landed here in 1432 and started trading with the local chiefs. During the War of the Castilian Succession, a naval battle between the Spanish and the Portuguese was fought just off the coast, in 1478, which resulted in the Treaty of Alcáçovas the following year, which gave a large part of South America to the Spanish, and the Portuguese gained control over trade in West Africa and particularly along this coast, comprising trading in pepper, ivory, gold and slaves.

Their primary interest was gold, with eight thousand ounces shipped to Lisbon from 1487 to 1489, twenty-two thousand five hundred ounces from 1494 to 1496, and twenty-six thousand ounces from 1497 to 1500. But the slave trade was starting and by 1535, over twelve thousand slaves had been transported from Elmina.

Then, in 1637 the Dutch West India Company captured Elmina and held it until control passed to the English in 1872, who had bought the area from the Dutch and then controlled it until independence in 1957. Until England abolished the slave trade, this was a major slave trading town, with slaves being brought from the hinterland and ships of various nationalities buying slaves and transporting them to the Americas.

However, the slave trade was not confined to those countries that had colonies in Africa. The book titled Ships of Slaves by Thorkild Hansen is a fascinating book detailing some of the involvement of Danish and Norwegian ships in the slave trade. It also details one particular Danish captain's involvement in shipping trade goods to Africa to buy slaves and gold, and then moving on to the Caribbean, before returning to Denmark with sugar, rum and tobacco; and more importantly, how these voyages made him rich and enabled him to move up the social hierarchy.

The major industries in Elmina now are tourism, fishing and the production of salt in the salt pans that surround the town which can be seen from the battlements of the forts. It was here that we said farewell to Martin, who was going further along the coast to stay in the Cape Coast before flying home to Sweden.

The next day was designated a truck cleaning day. It was hot dirty work to empty the truck, brush all the dust out, and then wash everything. We all had dedicated jobs, but the outside jobs were the coolest. Rowan and I sweated in the heat and in the confines of the truck, to get the dust out of the seats and wipe down every surface. Once it was dry, then everything had to be put back. We were having more people join us in Accra, so we had to empty one of the wood lockers so that it would be free for two of the newbies.

Our next sojourn was a few nights at Big Milly's Backyard on the beach near Accra. This is a great place, with a bar, live bands and two restaurants. Here, we said goodbye to Luis and welcomed our next four newbies. Imbe and Chris from Australia, (Chris was originally from the United Kingdom but he now had an Australian passport) and another couple, Gavin from Scotland and Elle from Ireland, both locum vets.

I had barracuda for lunch, but unlike my previous tasting of barracuda, these were two small whole fish. I had gone back to the same restaurant with the group and ordered my evening meal at seven p.m. and I was sitting by myself when my order finally arrived at eight thirty p.m. The waitress did come over and told me a couple of times that my order was coming, but it was still very late and by then, the others had finished and had gone off to the bar.

We were staying for some time in Accra to get several visas, so we had to travel into the centre of the city. The traffic was bad and despite having two or three lane roads, there was still a lot of congestion. The twenty kilometre journey took two hours, which is a similar time to the time it took to negotiate some of the mud tracks we had used to get through the jungle. We started at the Angolan embassy. It took three hours to take our biometrics, our finger prints and our photos and to hand in our forms. We wanted the passports back the same day to start the process to get visas for Togo and Benin, but the Angolan embassy needed to keep the passports with the applications. So, we returned to Big Milly's Backyard.

The next day, our visas were ready, but we didn't all need to go in person to collect our passports from the Angolan embassy, so Kim and Noodles took a taxi to collect the passports from the Angolan embassy and then ferry them and more forms to the Benin embassy. The two embassies are close together, so collecting our passports from one and taking them around the corner to hand them in to the next embassy took a quarter of an hour. But it took the taxi two hours to get into the centre and another two and a half hours to return to the campsite.

The rest of us had the day to ourselves to sit on the beach, to read or to relax and do nothing. After a lazy day at the beach, Conall and some of the others stayed up chatting at the bar until four a.m. but I finally got to my bed at midnight; but an hour before sunrise, the local preacher starting his morning service over the tannoy, plus the muezzin was calling the faithful to prayer. The night porters were up as well, sweeping the grounds and emptying bins, whilst the gardeners were watering the plants. There were upgrades available, but I was camping, and canvas has no sound proofing attributes, so I got up and I was washed, dressed and I was reading a book by six a.m.

I went with Kim to the Benin embassy to pick up passports and to take them and the completed application forms to the Togo embassy. But having handed the clutch of passports and forms to the officials, they told us that the embassy was closed till the following day, but the visas would be ready at the end of the day. We spent the day in the centre kicking our heels until everything was ready, and we returned to the camp, stopping off at an internet café, so that Kim could take photocopies of the visas for security. One thing I noticed as I travelled through the city is that unlike many other busy African cities, the drivers here don't constantly hoot their horns. Elsewhere, there is a constant symphony of car horns, but here they are rarely used.

I had had several nights camping, during all of which I had been woken up by the muezzin, the preacher and the hotel staff doing their chores. Therefore, for my last night at Big Milly's, I obtained an upgrade to a room for the night. It was a rondavel, a circular mud hut but made of brick and thatched with reeds. I had a double bed to myself. It was en suite, with a toilet and a shower around the back and they had a curious feature as there were walls but no roof, and it was open to the elements. Inside, under the table were a pair of electric sockets so that I could recharge my laptop, phone and cameras at leisure. The alternative would be to sit at the bar watching them charge, which was another reason why the bar was so popular.

We drove out of Accra and then it was back to familiar jungle scenery. It was still dry season; there was dust everywhere and smoke from the many small fires that produced a haze plus many black smuts, falling out of the sky.

We stopped at Akosombo, the town below the dam, which also gives its name to the dam. The Akosombo Dam is a rock filled embankment dam that was completed in 1966 and straddles the Volta River. It is a hundred and fourteen metres high and six hundred and sixty metres long across the top of the dam. It created Lake Volta which is the largest man-made body of water by surface area in the world, and the third largest by volume. Our guide was Tina, who took us on a tour around the dam to view the tailgates and the penstocks. There are six turbines, but they have only used a maximum of four at any one time and usually they only have two working. It has a capacity of 1,020MW and was conceived to provide electricity for an aluminium smelter at Tema, seventy kilometres away, on the coast.

Ghana takes twenty percent of the power generated, which meets seventy percent of local power requirements. Some is also exported to neighbouring Togo and Benin. The balance goes to the aluminium smelter.

But it is not all good news. More than eighty thousand people had to be rehoused, many of them subsistence farmers, and several settlements were built to rehouse them. The land surrounding the lake is not as good quality wise as the land in the valley bottom that is now flooded, and agricultural production has dropped. The increase of weeds in the lake has provided habitats for black fly, mosquitoes and snails, and an increase in water borne diseases such as malaria, bilharzia and river blindness.

We crossed the river downstream of the dam and drove north. We stopped en route for a bush camp in the grounds of a newly extended guest house. The new part was a three-storey modern design, which greatly expanded the hotel's former capacity of eight rooms, so the owner was confident of guests, but had not yet opened the extension.

I was on cook group and it was late, so I needed to start cooking. It was the newbies first bush camp, so they were guided through all the different jobs that needed to be done. I would worry about the tent later, as I could put it up in the dark. As it happened, there were upgrades available at a very reasonable rate, so I got a room with a shower and a toilet and a good night's rest without having to put up or take down the tent.

Our next stop was an eco-lodge next to the entrance to Wli Waterfall, run by a German couple who had been running the place for more than a decade. The waterfall here is the highest in Ghana, and the second highest in West Africa. There are walks marked, but the rules stipulate that you must have a guide, adequate footwear and enough water. They also offer walking poles, but I preferred not to bother with them but they seemed insistent that I take one, but I still refused. I wanted to do the Loop Walk which is advertised as a six hour long walk through the park, to arrive at the top of the waterfall and then a steep descent to the bottom.

I set off in the early morning, with my guide who introduced himself as Mawuli. The name means 'There is a God'. He was in his teens and probably did the walk several times a week. I am usually a fast walker, but he was bounding ahead of me on long slender legs, so he had the advantage of both youth and fitness.

We climbed up a steep hill with views across the valley and the plains far below. From part way up, I had a good view of the falls in the distance, as the water tumbled over the edge and cascaded into the plunge pool below. But we stopped only for a moment and Mawuli was off again. He set a fast pace and I struggled to keep up. I had done little exercise as I travelled over the previous three months, but he did the walk up to the waterfall at least once a day or perhaps twice a day, if he got back early he could take another group up.

The route curved upwards and across a dip and then followed a ridge to bring us out at the top of the falls. We passed through several different types of vegetation from jungle, to grassland and alpine pasture. Then we came to the falls. There are two sections, the upper falls and the lower falls. We clambered down to stand at the base of the upper falls. I had swimming trunks, but the water was cool, and the pool not inviting, but it was majestic to see the water cascading over the edge high above us into the pool.

It was a short way down, to stand at the top of the lower falls and to gaze down into the valley far below. The route then headed up the side of the valley and we worked our way along the valley side and then down to the bottom of the lower falls. I passed some of the others coming up on one of the shorter, less demanding routes. It is hard work going up and they wanted to know how much further it was, and whether it was steep and similar queries. Yes, it is steep, hot requiring large leg muscle jarring steps and still a way to go … all the wrong answers, so I was vague about details so as not to dispirit them.

I reached the bottom of the lower falls. All the way down, Mawuli was often out of sight. There were steep steps and boulders which I negotiated at my own pace. He did it regularly and probably just jumped, but I took my time as I wanted to get down in one piece. Every now and again he would call out, "Are you coming?" and I would answer, "Yes." He did it so often that I varied my response from, "Just taking a photo," "Having a pee," and even, "I have broken my leg" to which he said, "You are a brave man, I can still hear you walking through the jungle."

At the base of the lower falls I paid him off, and he went off with another guide, back to the entrance to find another group to guide. Meanwhile, I went for a swim in the lower plunge pool. It was shallow in places and you could wade out to stand underneath the plunging water standing waist deep. But not for long, as the falling water creates its own downdraught so it is windy, and the water falling on your head from a great height hurts after a while.

I walked out of the valley and through the entrance, past the inevitable souvenir stand. I was looking for black wooden elephants. My grandfather was a diplomat and, on his travels, he had collected a herd of black wooden elephants complete with tusks. There were several sizes and sexes, and in several different poses, all spread out along a window sill in his house. I clearly remember the herd and I often played with them as a child.

When he died, both my father and my uncle wanted them, so the herd was divided between the two sons. When my father died, my brothers and I also all wanted the elephants. Therefore, they were divided up again and I passed my share of the animals to my daughter. They are interesting but it is far from the herd that I remember as a child. Therefore, I was on the lookout for some additions. There were some, but they were rather crude and identical, so I didn't buy any, and I walked back to the eco-lodge.

CHAPTER 12
TOGO

The eco-lodge and the village were on the border, so it was just a ten-minute drive and then through emigration. There were only a few houses on the other side of the border and then the tarmac road ended, and it was a bumpy track up into the hills. There were several steep hairpin bends to negotiate, as we climbed into the hills. We stopped where there was some wood at the side of the road, to replenish our wood supplies. They were rounds of hardwood and it took a lot of effort to cut and to split them. Eventually, we just put whatever we could carry into the wood locker and we would split it later when we got to camp.

At the top of the mountain climb there was an upland plateau and a village. There were small fields and small plantations of bananas planted in patches of cleared forest. Some of the fruiting trees and valuable timber had been left when the land was cleared, so there were fields with trees standing in the middle of them.

After cresting a ridge, the road changed to a good tarmac road again and after a few more villages, the mountains gave way to hills and the road descended towards the plains, and our next destination of Lomé, the capital of Togo, where we would be camping on the beach.

The country was visited by the Portuguese, who established a trading post here in 1490. From the sixteenth century onwards, slaves were the main export and the area was known as the Slave Coast. It became a protectorate of Imperial Germany in 1884 during the scramble for Africa. It was invaded by the French during the First World War, and it became a French colony in 1918.

We were here not just to see the capital, but also to visit the Gabon embassy. When you are overlanding and on holiday, there is a tendency to let standards slip a bit. We looked rather scruffy, unshaven, no haircuts for a couple of months, sandals or flip flops, bare knees, bare shoulders, shorts or short skirts and whatever was comfortable and cool. We didn't want to look like hippies to people in authority in embassies, as no visa meant no more journey. Therefore, we tried to dress up a bit for embassy visits. So, on an embassy day, the gentlemen had to wear long trousers, and everyone had to have their shoulders covered. Some of the Muslim countries that we had come through might have objected to our first choice of clothing and could have refused a visa. That wasn't an issue necessarily for Gabon, but we had fallen into a routine. An embassy day meant trousers and shoes, blouses and at least a knee length skirt.

It took barely an hour to get our Gabon visas, and then we were free to get the next visa. We weren't required to appear in person at the Congo embassy, so Kim and Noodles headed off to the Congo embassy with our passports and our completed application forms, and the rest of us went into Lomé. It was often Noodles who joined Kim as she was Canadian and spoke fluent French, so if there was ever an issue at the embassy, it would not be because of a language barrier.

The truck went back to camp and the rest of us went for a boat trip and visited the fetish market. The boat trip was rather uninspiring, and the fetish market was expensive to get into, and small. I had seen a better fetish market in Kumasi. Voodoo is the main religion here, basing its beliefs on the power of the dead.

There were also protests planned for the Wednesday and the Thursday, in the centre of the city. The opposition's main request is for incumbent Faure Gnassingbé to leave power after taking over from his father, Eyadéma Gnassingbé after his sudden death in 2005. The former president Sylvanus Olympio was assassinated by Eyadéma Gnassingbé in January 1963. There was a military government followed by elections but Eyadéma staged a coup in January 1967 and his family have ruled ever since. Eyadéma Gnassingbé has the distinction of being one of Africa's longest serving leaders, staying in power for thirty-eight years and he rubs shoulders with other long-term leaders who have ruled for thirty-eight years, such as Robert Mugabe of Zimbabwe and Teodoro Obiang of Equatorial Guinea.

Faure Gnassingbé's current mandate was secured in 2015 and it runs till 2020 but the opposition disputes the validity of the elections and is calling for an immediate end to the Gnassingbé dynasty rule. The protests are peaceful but there is always a chance that the security forces might stage a crackdown, so they are best avoided.

We had a free day, but Rowan and I were on cook group duties and we had to go shopping. The markets were in the centre of the city, but we had spotted a local supermarket and a small stall selling vegetables at the side of the road, which had a wide selection. Rather than get a taxi into the centre with the associated time and expense and the impending protests, we would get whatever we needed from the local shops.

Rowan and I walked down the road to buy some beans, wraps, cheese, carrots, onions, pineapple, papaya, bread, eggs and a selection of salad items. In the heat of the late morning it seemed a long way and even longer coming back, with heavy shopping bags under a fierce sun.

It was just half an hour to the border with Benin. Travelling through Togo and Benin doesn't take long as they are barely eighty kilometres wide by the coast. The border was just thirty-seven kilometres away, along the coast road from Lomé.

CHAPTER 13
BENIN

We cleared Benin immigration and customs in seemingly no time at all and were soon at our next campsite at Grand-Popo by mid-morning. We were camping in the grounds of a hotel and a beach resort. I checked out the facilities, toilets, showers and the clothes washing area, plus the reception, bar and the restaurant. The upgrades for a room were expensive, so I would be camping again. I had enough time to put up my new mosquito tent for the first time since I had bought it in Accra. But it was too windy to leave it up. It was flimsy but cheap, and perhaps more designed to be used in the home, but as long as it lasted until the end of the journey in a few months, then I would be happy with the cost.

Benin was formerly the Kingdom of Dahomey and part of the Slave Coast. The kings traded slaves and thousands of war captives were sold as slaves and the kings of Dahomey became rich. Slave trading took a downturn after 1808, when Great Britain and the United States abolished the slave trade. The last slave ship left Porto Novo in present day Benin in 1885 for Brazil, where slavery was not yet illegal. France took control of the area in 1892 and in 1899, they renamed it French Dahomey and absorbed it into French West Africa.

I went on a tour of Grand-Popo with a French speaking guide and a translator. Many of the buildings were empty and abandoned. The guide said that it was due to sea encroachment that had swallowed some of the fields. Now the beach is at the edge of the village. However, the translator said that it was as a result of fighting during one of the coups that occurred in the country and subsequent political interference.

We got into a pirogue to move along the river and we were propelled by one of the boatmen, using a pole to push us along. We saw some mangrove swamps and saw several of the fish traps that locals use to catch fish, crayfish and shrimps. There were also lots of swifts and kingfishers flying up and down the river.

We landed on the far side of the river and walked through a local village. There was a voodoo shrine to a deity who looked after the village called the Labour, who would shout out to wake the locals up if a slave trader came near. There was also a voodoo religious site, but only those who had been initiated were allowed inside. There was another shrine and we were shown a particular type of tree. It is a good hard wood to build boats and houses, but by local superstition, the locals never cook with it. There was an option to watch a voodoo ceremony, but I declined, not due to the price, but I didn't want to perpetuate the beliefs or be involved in it, even as a spectator.

On the beach is a turtle sanctuary with four types of turtles including some leatherbacks. For a donation, we could release some of the baby turtles. I declined as they should be released at night, so they can evade predators as they cross the beach and from larger fish in the sea.

I was up early to shower before getting breakfast ready. The showers were in another block behind the hotel. There was no hot water, but I had become used to cold showers. I was halfway through my shower when the electricity cut out. There was only a small window above my head and it was still dark outside. I fumbled around in the dark until eventually, I opened the door to let in some feeble light from the grey dawn to collect my wash kit and to get dressed by.

We drove forty kilometres up the coast to Ouidah, a former slave trading town. The Portuguese reached here in 1580 and the British built a fort here in 1650. It was a major slave trading port and by the early 1700s the city was the second largest slave trading port along the Slave Coast.

The fort is now a museum although some of the original buildings have been demolished. It is only a small museum, but it does depict some of the history of the kings of Dahomey and the slave trade, with reproductions of paintings showing various contemporary scenes. There is also a reproduction of an iconic picture showing how the slaves were packed into the holds of the ships.

The picture is part of the story of the British Royal Navy's anti-slavery blockade of Africa in the early and mid-nineteenth century. The sloop-of-war the *HMS Primrose* with eighteen guns, under the command of Captain William Broughton captured the twenty gun Cuban slave ship *Veloz Passagera*, under the command of Jozé Antonio de la Vega.

The action took place off the coast of São Tomé and Príncipe, starting in the evening of the 6th of September 1830. The British attacked and boarded the Cuban vessel the next day. It was one of the few naval actions during the blockade but it was significant in terms of the forces and personnel involved. Forty-three slavers out of the crew of a hundred and fifty were killed in action and another twenty were wounded whilst the British lost three killed and twelve wounded. The *Veloz Passagera* had five hundred and fifty-six slaves aboard her when the *HMS Primrose* intercepted her. Only five slaves were killed during the action and the rest were freed from slavery.

Also, in the town is the Python Temple where there are several pythons. The legend is that the King of Dahomey was defeated whilst fighting another tribe and he ran into the forest to hide. When soldiers came to find him, the pythons wriggled out of the forest and protected him from the searching troops. Therefore, he honoured them by building a hut for them and they have been revered ever since. They are well fed, and it is safe to pick them up to pose for a photo. Some of the snakes sometimes escape but also some are intentionally allowed to escape to feed on rats and rodents, but they also eat bird chicks and pets. In turn, the snakes are safe and as it is said it will bring you bad luck if you kill one. It is thought to be a good omen to have a python in the house. Whenever the locals find one, they return it to the temple.

There is a four-kilometre walk from the site of the slave market passing by a large old tree, to the coast where the slaves would be loaded onto ships. The walk is lined with about twenty stations with statues mostly of mythical creatures, voodoo and slave related themes.

The rulers hadn't always traded in slaves but realised that they could make a lot of money from the trade and so they allowed it, and they actively participated in it. They would raid neighbouring tribes or buy the slaves from caravans and from other tribes. There were also war prisoners, abducted victims, and refugees from drought and famine.

The people also believed in voodoo and the slave traders used it to control and to subjugate the slaves. There is the Tree of Forgetfulness en route to the sea. Men walk around it nine times, women seven times, and it is said to induce amnesia for their country of birth, and that it would ensure that their soul would return to their home village.

Overlooking the sea at the end of the walk is the 'Gate of No Return', a large modern arch dedicated to more than twelve million slaves who were taken to the Americas. No formal records were kept, but that is the conservative estimate. Other estimates range up to twenty million.

There were often only a few guards. On the ships, the slaves would easily outnumber the crew and so, if they became organised, they could resist and escape. Hence the use of chains and shackles plus fear and voodoo.

A short walk away is the Hotel Diaspora and a camp site. It had a large swimming pool surrounded by a high single storey structure, designed to provide shade for the bathers. There were stairs going up to the flat roof for those who wanted to sit or lie in the sun. After a hot walk we were all tempted by the clean cool water of the swimming pool. There was a café selling refreshments but when we wanted to pay, they accepted our money but claimed not to have any change. It was a common practice and we had been caught out before. The seller I suspected, hoped that you would leave without your change. We tried to give them the exact money, but it is difficult when you never seem to get any change back. Our two options were either to ask the money changers for smaller denominations which wasn't successful as they rarely had smaller value notes, or to buy more goods to the value of the change, but you would then end up with some unwanted items.

We moved along the coast to Cotonou. The town is on the coast and just behind it is a large shallow lake. We planned to catch a boat to get to a stilted village that stands in the lake. The lake is on average two and a half metres deep. The area is rich in fish and fishing is the major activity there. Palm fronds are pushed into the soft sediment at the bottom of the lake to corral fish and to make it easier to catch them.

The village comprises several huts standing in the water. There are thoroughfares between the huts, with roads replaced by channels. Most of the houses had a boat tied up outside. There are also stilted shops, bars and hotels. In front of the largest hotel is an open area which serves as a floating market, where traders sit in their boats with their goods for sale; vegetables, fruits, shoes, clothes and the like. We stopped for refreshments at the hotel. There was no mains sewage and the toilet was just a hole in the floor. The fish have learnt that there may be easy meals to be had. Whenever anything hits the water, loads of fish rush in to eat whatever has just fallen in.

It is a fully functioning village with churches, hospitals, river police and a mosque. The fish that are caught are taken across the lake to the ferry port where there is a large market with several fish stalls.

We then had a long drive up country with an overnight bush camp. There was a lot of wood available, so after setting up the kitchen, we went hunting for fuel. There were some large pieces available that needed several people to drag them back to the camp, and then we could use axes and a chainsaw to cut it into smaller pieces for packing into the wood locker.

I rearranged my stuff and I filled up half my locker with firewood. I still had a half full bag of pine cones that were useful when we had no paper or cardboard to start a fire. We could use grass, but it didn't always burn well enough and produce enough heat to get the kindling going. As it was, when we packed up in the morning, we couldn't take all the wood that we had collected with us. We left a few bits that were awkwardly shaped such as bits where branches had split or bits with knots. Also, we left some of the smaller bits, preferring the larger logs as those are better for producing embers for cooking.

On our second day driving up country, we passed a series of hills. Oddly, they only appeared on the right-hand side of the road. They appeared as a child would draw hills; with steep sided cones, sometimes ending in a point, but as often as not, steep sides with a dome on top. Some of the sides were just bare rock and so steep that there was no vegetation on the sides. In contrast, the scenery around them was flat as it had been for several days through Benin and Togo. These were the first hills that we had seen since crossing the Togo border.

There was little traffic on the road but there were quite a few large lorries transporting cotton from the north to a processing plant in the south. But we had not seen any cotton fields, although the crop would have been harvested some time before.

We stopped in Parakou for an hour. It is a large Muslim town so we could not find any beer but there was plenty of fruit and vegetables and it was cheap. And we found tofu for the vegetarians. It was very hot with temperatures up to thirty-seven degrees Celsius. There were several mosques but some of the street traders were praying in the road next to their stalls, both men and women taking a break from commerce to pray.

We had difficulty finding diesel, but we persevered, and after the fifth station we found some. We passed through some villages and finally saw some of the mounds of cotton waiting to be transported southwards. The crop was sitting in big piles on flat ground, on the outskirts of the village. There were several piles but no markers so there was no indication as to whether they belonged to one farmer or to a cooperative.

Then came the drive north to find a bush camp and we found a quarry not far from the border. It had been sometime since we had last camped in a quarry, but it was a hole in the ground to hide the truck with some flat ground for the tents, although it was hard ground for tent pegs or digging a hole, but it was also waste ground, so it would be most unusual if someone were to object.

I didn't put up my main tent, I just unrolled the ground sheet, used the unrolled tent as a mattress and put up the mosquito net above the unrolled tent. It was hot during the day, but the temperature dropped during the night. I had to put on my fleece during the night, which I had been using as a pillow and I had to cover my feet with a tee-shirt.

CHAPTER 14
NIGERIA

Usually leaving a country is much easier than getting in, but the Benin authorities had their regulations and they wanted us to fill in departure forms. Then it was a hundred metres down the road to Nigeria and more forms to complete, a police interrogation, have our visas scrutinized and a check on the stamps that we had been given by another official just minutes before. Then came a visit to the department of health to check our yellow fever inoculation certificates. Lastly, we were asked about any fresh fruit, fresh vegetables and any meat. Luckily, we had no fresh meat, just some tinned pork luncheon meat which we had forgotten about, and so we hadn't had a chance to declare it, so we were guilty of breaking some regulation, but this was not discovered.

We would be in Nigeria for at least two weeks so we would have to change quite a bit of currency, and exchange our left over Ceefas. There were more visas to collect and to pay for, but this was difficult to budget for as we were not aware of the exact cost. The money changers were happy to change Ceefas and US dollars but they didn't want to change any euros so some people were unlucky. But, in the spirit of co-operation we lent one another some local currency until we could find a bank or a bureau de change.

Somehow, we were yet again very low on water, so we had to find the local village well. The money changers who had just had a bumper day changing loads of money directed us to a well outside the town and we stopped to fill up.

We had eighteen jerry cans, each holding twenty five litres, but only one was full. We had been using a lot of water, as we were eating off the truck three times a day, so washing up three times a day and it was hot, so we were drinking more, to ensure that we were hydrated, but it ate into the water supplies.

We were then able to get back on the road and head east towards Abuja, the capital of Nigeria. We had purposefully driven north up Benin and avoided the coastal border crossings, which would be busy, and the chaos of traffic around Lagos. We hadn't gone far when we came to a town and a turning to Kaiama. That was when the road turned from tarmac to dust. Suddenly, we were going at twenty kilometres an hour and making little headway. Having spent so much time sitting around at borders and filling jerry cans, we really wanted to get some distance under our belts.

We bumped along and eventually, despite the aspirations of getting some serious distance covered, we had to find a bush camp. We tried one turn, but it was a false trail into the jungle, and it stopped at a dead end. The trail was still being carved into the jungle as the local people sought out new sources of wood or perhaps some flat fertile land or perhaps access to a piece of land that someone had bought recently. What I really wanted to know, and I had never received an authoritative answer to my question on land ownership and the clearing of forests. What permits were required? How much did it cost? or did illiterate farmers just clear a patch of forest and it became theirs whilst they farmed it? I would never find out.

We then found another opportunity for a bush camp. It was low lying, and it would flood in the rainy season but in the dry season it was a long flat area, which offered a route deeper into the jungle, so we took it and we found a rather cramped spot, but it was flat, it had plenty of wood and it was sheltered from local villages and from the main track.

It was sheltered but it was another cold night and I was awake early as it was cold. At the next village there was a police check. Just a hundred metres further on was another and another. There were five checks within the same village, and I am sure that you could see the next check point from the previous one. One of two policemen at the check point asked us for water. We offered to fill his bottle up from one of our jerry cans. That wasn't what he wanted. He said that he could get water from the well, but he wanted some spring water which we didn't have.

We repeated our offer, but he made it obvious for us by saying that perhaps we could provide him with something to go shopping with for himself – that is a bribe, such an ugly word and it was never actually used. We apologised and we said that we couldn't help him.

He said, "You don't understand, a little something so that I can go to the shops." I knew perfectly well that he was asking for a bribe. Again, a smile and an apology and it was an impasse. He tried again and I smiled and said sorry again. He was not getting anywhere, so he let us go.

It was a very bad road, less of a track and more of a gully nearly all the way. Added to the discomfort, it was very dry and dusty. There were several bush fires off to the sides. Some areas had crops planted amongst the trees, and other areas were just forest. The rock beneath the ground poked above the surface in places, so some areas were never going to be cultivated.

Finally, at five p.m. we got to Kaiama, it had taken all day to travel eighty-two kilometres, but with some comfort breaks and police checks. Gareth and Kim got out at a police check, and then we all got out as well and we had a friendly chat with the police. They asked us where our escort was as there are terrorists in the bush who threaten the locals who are afraid to go too far into the bush. They patrol in the bush and they had come back to rearm. They never mentioned the Boko Haram by name, but there are militant Muslim extremists who control some areas of the north east of Nigeria, and parts of neighbouring Chad and northern Cameroon. It is one of the deadliest terror groups. It is most remembered in the west, for the mass abduction of two hundred and seventy-six school girls in Chibot in April 2014. Five years later, one hundred and twelve of the girls are still missing. Tens of thousands have been killed, and an estimated 2.3 million people have been dislocated from their villages.

The next checkpoint was only a few hundred metres away and it was visible from the previous one. We were stopped again and as we had spent some time chatting at the previous checkpoint, so they thought that we had been negotiating a bribe, and they wanted to know what we had given them. We hadn't given them anything, only the time of day and a look at out papers. And so, we went on. We were becoming used to police road checks and being asked for, "Something to go shopping with," but we never handed anything over.

Later in the day, we were stopped again by a group of young men, armed, in casual clothes and only one had a lanyard around his neck with the words 'Task Force' on it. It seemed doubtful that they were legitimate, so Kim asked for their ID, and the boss man went to the small hut at the side of the road and pulled out a laptop case. Inside was a police ID, and he handed it to Kim. It really was an ID, so we answered his questions and we were allowed on our way. But a lack of a uniform wasn't conclusive proof that they are not in authority.

We stopped in Wawa and it was stressed that we had a long drive ahead of us, and as we had just half an hour there, we had to hurry. The eggs were expensive, and we didn't find any ice, so we didn't buy any meat, but even that stretched the budget. Conall and Stefano missed departure time. We waited five minutes but had to move on, so Kim stayed behind, and Gareth drove a few kilometres down the road to find water and to fill up the jerry cans. Conall and Stefano met up with Kim and they paid for a taxi to catch up to us. We drove on reunited, but it was rude of them to be so late back, and they made no apology for delaying us.

We crossed the Niger River at Jebba just downstream of a dam, one of three massive hydroelectric plants that powers Nigeria. It is also home to Nigeria's largest paper mill which uses the power generated from the dam. It was still the dry season and several fires burned out of control at the side of the road. Along the main road, there must have been a petrol station run by every petrol retailing company in Nigeria. There was one every hundred metres for kilometre after kilometre. There was a lot of commercial traffic, but it seemed to be mainly petrol tankers, cow transports and scrap metal.

It was still two hundred and sixty kilometre to go, to Abuja. We bush camped in the forest as the next part of the road was either built up or were farmers' fields all the way to Abuja. It was good agricultural land with small squares of fields, as far as the eye could see. We stopped for lunch under a tree and we bought honey from a passing local. He had a bucket of the stuff plus some honey comb floating on the top. He poured a little honey into a water bottle and it held together as it sank to the bottom which is a sign that it has not been diluted and is therefore a sign of quality.

We had to queue for diesel as although Nigeria is a major oil producing country, distribution is difficult over such a large country, with some poor roads and where demand exceeds supply. There were several volcanic plugs standing proud from the surrounding ground. The roads improved and fifty kilometre short of Abuja, we picked up the motorway. Unlike the rural areas that we had come through, there were now lots of clean, new and expensive cars and lots of buildings, large up market residential semi and detached estates; and I noticed that many were gated communities. We wanted to get to the Cameroon embassy, but we would be too late, so we went to City Park, a sports club with a café, a restaurant, a cinema and somewhere to camp nearby. We were treated to a tour of the club led by the manager, Precious, who was very hospitable and welcomed us to his country. We were able to use their showers when they were open, but it would be busy in the afternoon as they were hosting several basketball playoffs.

The guidebook says that there is not much to do in Abuja, and despite trying to find something to see, the guidebook was right. And partly because of this, many locals leave the city at the weekend for their second homes, or to see friends and relatives.

We left early to be the first in the queue at the Cameroon embassy, when it opened at eight a.m. Unfortunately, and contrary to the website, it didn't open until nine-thirty a.m. Therefore, we had some free time and I stopped for a coffee at a local café. Again, just like Benin, Togo, Ghana and elsewhere, there was no change for the note that I offered, so I got a small bottle of water, as part of the change but I still ended up paying over the advertised price, but there was nothing cheap enough to make up the difference.

There were shops in the vicinity but nothing of interest to me. I had lost my head torch, and I couldn't find a replacement. We returned to the embassy which was now 'open' but not open to the public. A 'job's worth' official said that they would not accept our forms nor hold onto our passports over the weekend, and that we should return on Monday. I am sure that if I had flashed some cash there would have been a different outcome but that was not going to happen.

This was a bit of a blow, but we always had a Plan B. The alternative was not to waste the weekend in Abuja waiting for the embassy to open, but to go to their consulate in Calabar in the south east corner of Nigeria near the border with Cameroon.

Therefore, we went to the mall and did some shopping. I didn't find a camping shop, so I was still without a head torch. We returned to City Park for our evening meal, hosted by Precious in the sports bar, followed by an evening in the open-air cinema showing Thor.

We left Abuja to head south east to Calabar to get our Cameroon visas. We left the last of the suburbs and thinning residential areas and then we crossed sparse forest on rocky ground and through some steep-sided hills. Late in the day, we pulled off the road some distance south of McCafferty and drove a long way along a dirt track past many round huts. We were unable to do this surreptitiously, as we were in a large, noisy, yellow truck throwing up great clouds of dust. We pulled off into a field which had had a forest fire sweep through it, so the ground was charred and full of ash, but the larger bushes and trees had survived.

We had set up the kitchen and had started to cook, but we were soon surrounded by the locals who came in pairs. There were soon so many watching us that most of the village was there. It was the polite thing to do and so, we asked whether we could camp. There was a lot of banter amongst the locals and the village elder came forward and through one of the locals who spoke English, he said that we would have to ask the king. We spoke to his representative and he didn't appear to say no, but a messenger was sent to the king. One of the young lads ran off with a message.

Soon some motos arrived and three of us led by Kim went to go to see the king to plead our case and to ask for his permission. This took a while and the group ate the evening meal whilst waiting to hear the king's answer.

There were now more villagers, armed police and soldiers surrounding the group, watching us eat. The reply from the king was that we couldn't stay there. I wasn't sure whether it was a hospitality issue or whether he just wanted to be rid of the responsibility of hosting some uninvited European guests.

We packed away out tents and the kitchen and were escorted by the police with flashing blue lights, back up the track to the main road for a short distance, and then we were led into a compound on the side of the road. This was the compound where the district police commissioner lived, surrounded by high walls and twenty-four hour security, provided by some of his staff. He was also a prince in the local royal family, Prince Vincent Amaabal; so I suspect that the king had passed responsibility onto another member of his extended family.

We received a friendly welcome by the commissioner himself. We were shown were to set up camp in the compound and we were given a tour and shown the facilities. He was also generous enough to provide some cold beers and soft drinks and he refused any payment.

Later in the evening there was some music and dancing. We had a show of some local traditional dancing, and we were invited to join in. We were introduced to some members of his family and to some of his senior commanders, some in uniform, some in casual clothes, so sometimes it was difficult to understand who was family and who was part of the police hierarchy.

Some of them spoke seriously, saying that we had been in danger and that they could have come in the night with spears and machetes to see us off. There was a local problem with squatting refugees, but we hardly fitted the picture of a typical refugee from Cameroon. We were also told that the locals thought that we were slavers ready to capture them, so they may have attacked us in the night.

It had been a cold night and there were clouds in the sky in the morning. Unexpectedly we got fresh hot water, hot cassava and a hot spicy stew for breakfast. I had a chat with Prince Vincent Amaabal. He has four children who are all studying in Wolverhampton. He showed me pictures of several landmarks in both the Midlands and in London, and I was able to identify most of them, so we had something to chat about.

Whilst we were doing this, there were several subordinates who came to seek his opinion. They walked up, saluted and gave a verbal report. Sometimes the messenger was dismissed with a casual wave of the hand. Other times, orders were given, other people summoned, and instructions given. On one occasion, Prince Vincent's face turned serious, as a long report was recited, and several questions asked and answered. It was all in the local language, so I didn't understand the content, but something serious had happened and it needed urgent action. Ten troopers piled into two pickups and they roared out of the compound to attend to whatever was amiss.

I regret that I was too polite to ask what the problem was, but equally, I am sure that my host would have made it out to be a trifling matter and under control. But I also noticed that whatever was happening, that there was always another person constantly taking notes. He was inconspicuous and sat behind and to one side of Prince Vincent, but he was always there, and always scribbling. I assumed that this was his secretary or court recorder, but he was always within earshot.

We exchanged business cards and whilst it was a formality, and I am sure that he has a lot of contacts in the United Kingdom, but I would be only too happy to return his hospitality if he or his family needed assistance.

We were escorted from the compound where we had stayed by two Toyota pickups with troopers inside and more standing on the bumper and hanging off the back. We were escorted as far as the next police district. They peeled off but it was obvious that our arrival had been forwarded to the next checkpoint and we sailed through several army and police checkpoints without being stopped.

But we only had a smooth ride for a while as if the commissioners' rule only ran so far before we crossed into another jurisdiction. We got stopped several times at the next few checkpoints, and we were always asked for a manifest. We drove across the plateau and then came to some hills. This was the edge of the plateau and the road descended into a valley.

Beside the main road was a petrol station and we stopped for lunch. There were dark clouds above us and the tops of the mountains nearby were obscured. There were a few spots of rain, but the clouds hurried on to drop their rain somewhere else.

We turned off the main road, up a side road, through a village, forded a stream, and then we parked the truck on the outskirts of the village of Bounchor. This was where we were going to spend the night and visit a primate sanctuary. The bungalow opposite where we stopped was where one of the managers of the eco-lodge lived.

He welcomed us wearing a black tee-shirt with the picture of a gorilla on the front with underneath it, the slogan, 'My Gorilla, My Community'. The place where we parked was what would have been his lawn if there was enough rain to encourage the grass to grow. As it happened it was just a sandy flat area, devoid of plant life.

We were early but we had to walk to our camp as the road was too rough and too steep for the truck. Therefore, a pickup was coming down from the camp to pick up our gear, tents, kitchen, food, sleeping bags and personal items. It was a forty-minute walk but motos were available at a price, to take people up.

As there were some cafés in the village, it was suggested that we could spend some time in the village before going up to the camp. We pulled our gear out and sorted through the stacks of pots and pans, knives, spices and the like and to get our own personal items off the truck and the necessary kitchen equipment to leave them in a pile for the pickup to take up to the camp.

I was the first one to be ready and it was a very hot afternoon. The clouds had blown over and the sun was streaming down. It was a short walk back to the town, and I started out by myself. At the ford, a woman washing clothes called out that there was someone running after me shouting. I didn't recognise him, but I waited, and I greeted him.

He introduced himself as Chris and he said that he was a local guide who knew about the animals in the area. He spoke excellent English and worked part time at the animal sanctuary. We stopped at the first shop for refreshments. Even my water was warm, and it wasn't pleasant to drink tepid water, so the cold drink was very welcome. We chatted for a while and we spoke about the issues of conservation, the eco-lodge, local life, the border and Cameroon.

Some of the others came past and walked on and around the corner. Chris went off and I moved on from my corner shop to find the others. They were at another gathering point. I hesitate to call it a shop or a bar, but it was an open sided, roofed area that sold bread from a table opposite the road and beer from a freezer from around the back of a shed.

Esther served us and she was a colourful character who flirted with us, and we nicknamed her 'Esther the Molester'. Several people came past and stopped for a chat. Several of the locals worked at the eco-lodge. There was Raphael, who was a night guard, Takum, a general worker who was deaf and dumb, but managed to communicate with most people. There was Cobra who was on his way to work as a night guard for the chimpanzees. Many of the locals seemed to have indulged in drinking beer, and they were difficult to understand, as they slurred their words.

A little later Zac came and joined us. He was the young American manager of the centre, who had worked there for three years. He was on his way back from Calabar where the charity had an office and had returned to the centre after three months away 'doing paperwork'.

It was a convivial atmosphere, but it was time to get to the camp. Some would be going by moto but as I opted to walk, it would take forty minutes or more in the late afternoon heat, and I had a rucksack to carry, so I set off early. I wanted the exercise as I had done so little recently, other than just sitting in the truck.

As I was walking, I was passed a little later by Zac on the back of a moto, but after that I saw no one else. I walked for an hour and I still hadn't got to the Drill Ranch. However, coming down the road towards me were Conall, Stefano and Mikkel. They had walked for a long time and they had realised that they had missed the turnoff. I was also starting to think that I had also gone the wrong way, so I wasn't the only one. I was happy to turn around and retrace our steps and look for a sign at every turning.

We found a sign but only because we were actively looking for it. It was painted green, so it melded into the general colour of the jungle. It was also set back from the road on the edge of the jungle, so it was partly obscured and it was easy to miss. But at least it said Drill Ranch, so it was the right turning.

We set up the tents, the kitchen and we sorted out our personal belongings. Then we had the opportunity to walk around the camp site and the animal sanctuary. The toilet facility was down a path through the jungle. There was a piece of rope fixed to a tree to one side of the path. On the opposite tree was a nail and to indicate that the toilet was occupied, you tied one end of the rope to the nail and across the trail.

There was only a single toilet but there was plenty of jungle if it was occupied. It was a long drop with a porcelain bowl above a dark pit. The shower was down another path with a similar piece of rope to indicate whether it was occupied or not. As a camp site this was a relatively modern and robust affair. There was a sink and a drying area, a raised area made of bamboo to stand on, under a large shower head, enclosed by a wall of bamboo for modesty. Above, there was a large black plastic tank which could hold a thousand litres of water, which was reached by a set of stairs to one side of the structure. Unfortunately for all its modernity and its sophistication, there was no automatic filling up, so you still had to carry a bucket from the nearest tap to pour into the tank for it to flow down to the shower head.

In an enclosure on the way back to the centre of the eco lodge were four red eared guenon monkeys, with red ears and long red tails. They are indigenous and there are groups in the local area. These ones had been rescued and would be released into the wild in due course.

I still hadn't been able to replace my head torch and there were no lights at the centre or at the campsite, which doubled as a car park during the day. I had to borrow a head torch from Noodles, to see what I was doing. They obviously don't expect many visitors who bring their own car, as the car park had space for perhaps just four cars before it was full. Consequently, our nine tents took up most of the space, with just a small walkway between each one. In bush camps we usually spread out with at least a couple of tent lengths between each tent, so this felt cramped.

On our last morning we packed everything away and made a pile of tents, kitchen things and personal bags to be taken down the road by pickup back to the truck, whilst we had a tour of the centre. The first stop was the Drill monkey enclosure. These are an endangered species so the work done by the centre is critical to their survival. Their natural habitat is being encroached upon by a swelling population and farmers looking for new land to cultivate. Another animal – human conflict is that they also eat the farmers' crops so they may endanger themselves as they seek food sources that farmers have conveniently planted near to their normal foraging area. Logging activities, both legal and illegal are decimating their habitat, and without the trees for cover and for food, they need to move on or die. More people mean more hunters, who trap them alive, to sell as pets or for bush meat.

The sanctuary has several enclosures for the monkeys. The enclosure in front of us was over seven hectares in size and it contained a troupe of over forty monkeys, with a dominant male and several other males. They have distinctive red and blue bottoms and genitals. This group might be released into the wild further up the mountain if conditions allow, but that is always controversial, as there are conflicts of interest between farmers wanting to grow crops to survive, and conservationists who want remote areas to protect a species. Unfortunately, there are fewer and fewer areas that are remote, as population growth continues to put pressure on local land resources. Once upon a time, both groups could co-exist, but the human population is expanding so fast that soon there will be no remote areas for the animals to be left alone in.

Everyone in the village was super friendly and welcoming, all spoke English and we could converse without a problem. They also knew that the centre employed dozens of locals as wardens, keepers, and guards, and so they welcomed the employment opportunities that the centre provided.

Further away from the centre was the chimpanzee enclosure, spread over thirty-two hectares for thirty chimps. They have mixed origins, but they are all orphans. They will never be released as they are too domesticated and would not survive in the wild. The population is stable as the males have been castrated.

The centre was started in 1991 with just one animal. Originally it was partly funded by the Nigerian government but due to cutbacks and the withdrawal of funding, the centre now must be self-supporting. It is a massive cost to provide food for the six hundred Drill monkeys and the thirty chimps and a few other monkeys, but they just about manage. They have the eternal problem of whether to remain a scientific study centre, working on a shoestring or to become a tourist attraction, and with it gain a bigger income but then lose sight of their founding principles.

It was fascinating to watch the chimps. They are encouraged to come close to the viewing site by the rangers who bring a bucket of nuts to throw over the fence. There was the usual chimp behaviour and occasional fighting, with the dominant male enforcing his seniority on some of the other males. Some chimps were ignored, others were too busy eating to react to the fighting around them, and some seemed to be picked on more often than others. Some stood together to provide protection, screeching at an attacker, or they would co-ordinate an attack on the dominant male but would run off after an unsuccessful attack. Others picked up stones to use as tools to break open the nuts, or they used long twigs to pull the nuts that had fallen out of reach on the wrong side of the electric fence towards them. It was incredible to watch them interacting and exhibiting actions so like human behaviour.

There was plenty of time, so I opted to walk back along the track to get back to the truck parked on the outskirts of the village, checking a few side turnings into the jungle. Gareth was rotating the tyres and changing a couple to mud tyres, for better grip as the rains were coming, and Cameroon roads were notoriously poor. We were warned that progress might be slow, and it would be like some of our previous jungle tracks where eighty kilometres in five hours is considered good progress; and it can be a rough journey as the passengers get thrown around, and it is not possible to sleep or to read a book, but one had to just persevere.

We stopped at Ikom near the border with Cameroon on our way to Calabar. The border area is a problem area with security issues arising from tensions between the Anglo and the Francophone halves of Cameroon, which makes the border area dangerous, even on the Nigerian side, as there are more security forces there than normal, to cope with migrants, refugees and illegal border crossings. Therefore, we stayed at a hotel which had its own secure compound. It was a great upgrade with a bar, a restaurant, a swimming pool, a tennis court and lots of nice cars in the car park, plus UN, Immigration and Border Police and Red Cross vehicles.

The water went off during the night and they tried fixing it then and there. There was someone banging and clanking seemingly all night, and it was still not fixed in the morning when we left for Calabar. We drove through an agricultural area with fields and plantations of fruiting palm trees, coconuts, palm oil and rubber plantations.

We went straight to the Cameroon consulate and handed in our passports. They were super-efficient and said that the visas would be ready in just two hours. That was excellent service, so why couldn't other embassies match that sort of turnaround time? We had lunch on the truck just around the corner, whilst we waited, and then we headed off to Naks Hotel.

We were going to camp in the hotel grounds but the suggested location for the tents was a building site for a large extension and workmen were laying the foundations. It was noisy and dusty work. We had to wait until they had finished at maybe six or seven in the evening, before we could put the tents up. Meanwhile, we had the rest of the afternoon to ourselves. The town had a slave museum which I wanted to see, which was small but interesting, but I learnt little that I hadn't known already.

After so much bush camping it was great to have some upmarket facilities. It was a sprawling place with four bars and a swimming pool, which regrettably was murky. The staff were helpful, and I had paid extra for the internet, but only then did I find out that it didn't work, and there was a nil refund policy, so I was out of pocket.

The workmen left shortly after six p.m. and I put up my tent on the sand that was the first layer of the foundations. I walked out of the hotel to the local shops to find a restaurant. There was a selection of menus and one specialising in fish, so that was where I went to order, and I chose a table outside under an awning.

The rainy season started here at seven fifty-one p.m. I was sitting waiting for my meal and the heavens opened. There are no words to describe how heavily it rained or how noisy it is, as the rain beats down on roofs and awnings and the ground turns into a river. But anyone who has experienced a monsoon will remember the noise, the sheets of water flowing across the ground, and if you get caught without any cover, the heavy, persistent hurting rain.

I ate slowly and I had a drink at the bar next door, hoping that the rain would ease off, which it didn't. I stepped out into the rain and I was soaked to the skin within minutes. By the time I had arrived back to my tent, I felt that I had had a shower with my clothes on. I crawled into my tent and I went to bed wet.

It stopped raining during the night, but the tent was still wet. I packed it away wet, and we set off for the return journey to Ikom en route to the border.

CHAPTER 15
CAMEROON

This border crossing has a checker history. It was shut for two months in the autumn, and it can be shut at weekends and seemingly arbitrarily at any time, so we wanted it to be over as soon as possible. The roads in Cameroon were notoriously poor so the going would be slow as well. We would be going through an area where it is suggested to avoid all but essential travel.

It was an early start so I would have gone to bed early, but there was a party at the bar. It seemed that most of the hotel were at the bar and we mixed with some UN and Red Cross officials. They have certain travel restrictions imposed by their respective head offices, such as not leaving the hotel compound after dusk, so there is little else for them to do other than catch up with paperwork or go to the bar. The music was loud, and it continued well into the night. It was replaced during the night by someone near my room who had turned their TV up to full volume and it blared out all night. I could make out the actors' words and whilst I didn't recognise the dialogue, I recognised some of the actors' voices, and it was some old Hollywood blockbuster. Being that loud and in English, I found myself listening to it to get the thread of the storyline rather than getting back to sleep.

I also had another reason for not getting to bed early. I had spent three hours in the restaurant the night before. I had gone to the restaurant with Gavin and Elle. My first order for fish wasn't available. I chose Fisherman's Soup instead and the waitress disappeared. Mikkel had ordered an hour before us but Gavin and Elle's omelettes came out first and then, a little later, Mikkel's chicken arrived.

One of the waitresses walked past me and then stopped and turned to ask me why I was there. My answer was that I was waiting for my order, to which she replied that there was no other serving on order. The other waitress had forgotten my order. Therefore, I ordered an omelette hoping that it would be quick and easy and it wouldn't take long. However, it did take a while, and by then I was sitting in the restaurant by myself. My only company was Sarah, who had ordered a meal but was sitting outside. She too was experiencing a long wait and came in several times to check on the progress. She chatted with me until one of the waitresses came past. After my experience, Sarah would check with the waitress every time she passed to ensure that her order was still being worked on and had not been forgotten.

At breakfast we asked how people had slept. All of us had been kept awake, firstly by the loud music from the party at the bar, followed by the sound of somebody's television turned up to maximum volume, that blared out all night.

The cook groups had been rearranged and several people commented on Kenny's lack of contribution. He hadn't contributed to any ideas within his cook group and hadn't gone group shopping that day with the other members of his cook group. He was on cook group duties that morning and he should have been helping to set up the kitchen for a six a.m. breakfast. He turned up at six twenty a.m. despite the rule and precedent for the last few months being for breakfast to start one hour before departure, which would then last for half an hour, to allow the cook group to clear away. Whilst the cook group are responsible for clearing away, usually several people help. Without any apology for being late, Kenny helped himself to some cereal and then he left a partially eaten bowl of cornflakes on a chair and went to pack away his things from his room. The washing up bowls had been left out for Kenny to wash his bowl after he had finished, but everything else was put away.

A few minutes before departure, Gareth would start the truck which was usually the sign for us to get on board. Kenny came back, picked up his bowl and sat on the truck to eat his breakfast as we drove, thus avoiding both setting up and clearing away. We needed to get going so we had to pack away the washing up bowls for departure.

He had been told but he just didn't get it. My personal gripe on the point of leaving dirty plates on the truck all day was that they would not get washed until that evening, by which time the food had attracted flies and the remnants had dried solid, and it was a pain to get clean. And it was another job for the cook group setting up for the evening meal.

One of the girls commented that it wasn't unusual, and it was strange, but perhaps a situation of 'birds of a feather,' as Conall and Stefano were a clique with Kenny, but all of them were rarely seen washing up and clearing away after a meal. In Conall's defence, he rarely had breakfast, so, as he didn't get anything dirty, he might have felt that he was exempt from the breakfast routine. Stefano reacted to a chance aside from Gareth a few days earlier. We had been asked as a group to give the lunch time cook group a hand to set up, so that we could have a quick lunch and get on our way again as we had a long way to cover. Stefano was changing his footwear and most of the jobs had been done when Gareth walked passed and reiterated the need for everybody to contribute. Stefano retorted that he did contribute and that it was not a race. However, by the time he had his boots on, all the jobs had been done, so he had got away without doing anything, but the standard was for communal jobs to take preference for the benefit of the group, and then you had time to do your own thing.

It was under twenty kilometres to the border at Ekok, and we were there in plenty of time, but we had to fill out numerous forms just to leave the country, which seemed to take a couple of hours, so it was an opportunity to read and to relax whilst we were processed.

There is a bridge across the river which formed the border. It was only wide enough for one vehicle and there was no order imposed such as a one-way system with traffic lights. Drivers would get onto the bridge and bounce up onto the pavement, scattering pedestrians and cyclists to squeeze past one another.

We had a grandstand view of this from the truck, as we were parked facing the bridge, whilst we were processed. We were first in the queue to cross the bridge when there was a commotion on the bridge. People were jumping out of cars and running towards the Nigerian end of the bridge. Motorcyclists were turning around and heading back towards us. Pedestrians jumped onto the back of motos to get back. Drivers who had got on to the bridge from the Nigerian side, were reversing fast, back the way they had come. There was an air of panic. Drivers coming from the Cameroon side were saying that there had been firing and that people had been killed, and there was a general panic, with rumour and fear causing people to run away from the border.

Had there been any shooting we would have heard, as the bridge was less than fifty metres long, and we could see the border post on the far side. Where there had been a mass of people moving across the bridge, it was now empty. We could see the Cameroon armed border guards standing shoulder to shoulder in a line across the road, and nobody else on the far side.

The border authorities on our side had closed the border to Nigerians, but people from Cameroon could cross if they wished, but no one wanted to go. We had officially been stamped out of Nigeria, so they wouldn't allow us back into Nigeria. It was rather like being Tom Hanks in the film 'The Terminal' as we were stuck between countries. As non-locals who had been stamped out of Nigeria we could only go across the border, but we would only be allowed across once the authorities on our side had spoken to an official on the far side, to ascertain the situation.

It turned out that there had been a shooting in a nearby village during the night, but the news had spread by word of mouth and like Chinese whispers, the story became increasingly inaccurate. There had been a fire fight between the border forces and the militants, just weeks before, so the danger was real. In the tense border area where everyone was aware of security issues, someone had caused a panic and ran, sparking the mass panic.

The border was reopened, and we were the first across. The queue that had formed behind us had vanished as people decided to go home and to cross another day. We had more form filling to do to get into Cameroon. Whilst we waited a force of armed border guards deployed around us. They had black uniforms with BIR in large letters on their backs, signifying the Rapid Intervention Brigade (shortened to BIR in French). Their colonel parked his command vehicle near ours, and his troops deployed in a large circle around us, facing outwards. We didn't want to wait any longer than necessary, as we wanted to get as far away from the border as fast as possible.

Portuguese explorers reached the coast in the fifteenth century and named the area Rio dos Camarões, after the ghost shrimps that they saw in the river, which later became Cameroon in English. The first German involvement in the area started in 1868 when the Woermann Company from Hamburg built a warehouse on the Wouri River. Later Gustav Nachtigal made a treaty with one of the local kings to annex the region for the German emperor, and it became the German colony of Kamerun in 1884.

Development of the economy was based on concessions which used forced labour to create banana, rubber, palm oil, and cocoa plantations, and to improve the infrastructure of the colony. The use of forced labour was unpopular with the natives and it was criticised at the time by other colonial powers.

The colony was invaded by French, British and Belgium troops during the First World War and in 1922, the League of Nations handed out mandates splitting most of the country in to becoming a French mandate; and the western corner and a separate northern area were designated as a British mandate.

In 1960, the French-administered part of Cameroon achieved independent and it became the Republic of Cameroun. There was a UN sponsored plebiscite for the British Cameroons, with the northern mainly Muslim area opting to join Nigeria and the southern former British mandate and English-speaking area opted to join French speaking Cameroun.

In February 1984 the President of Cameroon Paul Biya changed the official name of the country from the United Republic of Cameroon to the Republic of Cameroon, the name that Francophone Cameroon held before its unification with Anglophone Cameroon; which was deeply unpopular with the English-speaking areas. They felt that their individual culture was being assimilated into French culture, and that the president had seceded from the sense of the 'United' Republic.

Writing in March 1985, the Anglophone lawyer and President of the Cameroon Bar Association Fon Gorji Dinka stated that the Biya government was unconstitutional and announced that the former Anglophone area should become independent as the Republic of Ambazonia. He was arrested and became a martyr for the Anglophone people's cause.

Since then, the Francophone area, comprising eighty percent of the population has increasingly marginalised the Anglophone speaking areas. Education is in French and aid and government spending is concentrated disproportionately in the Francophone areas. The independence movement is represented by the Southern Cameroons Peoples Organisation (SCAPO) and the area is called Ambazonia by the separatists.

In 2005, the Republic of Ambazonia joined the Unrepresented Nations and Peoples Organisation and is now one of its larger members by virtue of the numbers of people who they represent, along with other and better-known minorities such as Tibet and Kurdistan. Other members such as the Aboriginals of Australia are suspended, as they do not follow all the covenants of the organisation. Other members have left, due to recognition, autonomy or independence, such as Georgia, Armenia, Estonia and Latvia. Ambazonia declared its independence in October 2017, so it has a history and it is bold enough to carry on the struggle.

There are other problems facing Cameroon. It must deal with refugees and asylum seekers from Chad and the Central African Republic, and it has deployed troops to the west and to the northern borders to deal with the insecurity caused by Boko Haram. Corruption is endemic as it is in a lot of African countries. Human rights organisations claim that there are prisoners held without trial who are tortured. Political opponents claim that the elections are rigged.

Despite the guide book warnings, the road was brand new smooth black tarmac, with brand new shiny road signs, no potholes, no bumps and with a bright white line painted down the middle and down the sides. A Chinese company is building a new bridge and border control facilities, and they probably built the road as well. We made good time on the empty roads from the border to Mamfe.

We could have gone further, but we needed to find a bush camp and there was a chance that if the military found us, that we would have to move on, or they would insist that we camped in their compound, which wasn't attractive either if we were to get caught in any crossfire. Therefore, we stopped mid-afternoon in Mamfe at the local Roman Catholic Mission. There was flat grass to camp on, a bar and a restaurant, numerous clean toilets with paper, and several showers with hot water, so it turned out to be quite a nice discovery.

The road continued to be excellent all the way to Kumba. There was only one exception where the tarmac abruptly stopped and the road followed a diversion up the hill, next to a deep cutting that, from our vantage point high up the hill, had a gentle but flat curve through a deep cutting to come out high above a river, with a newly built two lane bridge over the river, and a sweeping road up the far side of the valley. Our diversion took us through a couple of hairpins past the end of the new bridge and then down to the old single-track bridge over the river. From here we could see the new bridge in all its majesty but there was no work going on and no machinery on site, not even a night watchman. The bridge looked finished and there was gravel on the intended route of the road. It only needed a covering of tarmac and it would be complete, but work seemed to have stopped.

Kumba was a reasonable sized town with a major road going south to join the coast road between Limbe and Douala. We had thought that this might take two days, and there were so many checkpoints with police or army all asking to see passports, check nationalities, look over the truck and so on, that we thought that we might not make it to Limbe. We had a sweepstake on how many checkpoints there would be.

At one check point there were women selling smoked fish by the roadside. I expressed an interest in tasting the fish, within earshot of the senior policemen who was standing nearby whilst one of his subordinates took down our details. He called over one of the women and Mat and I had a free tasting. It was pleasant and apparently the locals ate the bones as well, and I liked the flesh, but I thought that the bones were too hard and too large to be enjoyable.

The roads were so good that we could keep up a good speed, despite a few checkpoints and we arrived in Limbe in the late afternoon. Our beachfront location was in the grounds of the Mirabar Hotel, within the Botanical Gardens. It had two bars, a large swimming pool, an excellent award-winning sea food restaurant just ten metres away, and a marvellous location overlooking the sea, with some islands just off shore and incongruously for such a lovely spot, an oil drilling platform standing in shallow water with its legs reaching high above the deck, awaiting its next commission.

Our local fixer, Thompson, came to tell us about a climb on Mount Cameroon, the tallest mountain in West Africa at four thousand and forty metres. There were several treks on offer, and so Sarah, Rowan, Jacci and I signed up for a three-day hike which included some recent vents, calderas, fissures and lava fields, and a second night on the mountain, and then a long gradual descent. We would have a six-berth tent between the four of us.

I went shopping for supplies as departure was scheduled for six a.m. the next morning, and there would not be time to buy anything en route. We would have to carry our own food, so it was a trade-off between what we wanted to take and what we could comfortably carry. There was the usual tuna fish and pasta, but also a couple of bottles of wine to be added to the supplies.

The taxi was late, but it didn't matter, as Kingsley, our driver drove like a madman and made up time. Rowan was in the front and had a hellish experience as Kingsley drove around potholes, early morning joggers and parked lorries on the side of the road with no lights and the occasional goat. We didn't take the main road but took the old road instead. It was quieter but it was also more scenic. We passed field after field of tea bushes, part of the giant Cameroon Tea Plantations Company.

We picked up Thompson in central Buea. This was the capital of German Kamerun from 1901 to 1919, and the capital of British Cameroons from 1949 to 1961. There are several iconic and distinctive colonial era buildings, such as the palatial residence of the former German governor Jesko von Puttkamer, who was governor of Kamerun nine times between 1887 and 1906. There are several other modern buildings that have been built, with signs showing that they had been built with more recent aid from Germany.

There were already five adults squeezed into the car, so it was already cramped before Thompson got in. This is overcrowding in the United Kingdom but here in Africa there was space for probably another half a dozen, so the locals think nothing of it, but we were appalled that we were to be squeezed into such a small space.

Luckily, it was a short journey for us to get to our starting point of the trek. Some things had already been squashed and we had rescued a few such as some avocados and bananas, but we would find out later that we hadn't rescued everything.

We left our motley assortment of bits for the porters to sort and pack as they thought fit, and the four of us and our guide, introduced to us by Thompson as Brandan, started up the trail.

So, we started, me first, then Rowan, then Sarah and Jacci. It was a cool morning and at an elevation of a thousand and ten metres. It was a pleasant temperature as we walked up through fields. We passed an open prison which is where some of the vegetables are grown for the main prison, situated a bit further back down the road.

After the last field, it was a steady upward climb through the jungle. There was thick foliage and no air movement and as we climbed, we broke out in a sweat. After more than an hour we came to Hut Number One, where we stopped for a break, sitting on the veranda. There was little inside other than a single bed and a table, but no chairs. Around the back was some long drops and a shed. The hut could be booked for those who wanted to take the trek up the mountain at a slow, leisurely pace.

There were various options varying from one to six-day treks. There was a one-day option, but that started at three a.m. and after climbing up for eight hours to reach the summit, there was a long descent back the same way, and finishing in the dark, so it was only for very fit and committed trekkers who didn't have any spare time. The two-day option had a break at Hut Number Two which is at two thousand eight hundred and fifty metres but there is still a long climb to reach the summit at four thousand and forty metres and down again.

We set out from Hut Number One after a ten-minute break. Not far up the track was a large scattering of empty plastic bottles and discarded plastic wrapping. The day before had been the 27th Mount Cameroon Race for Hope run, which is a charity event to run up to the summit and back, covering thirty-eight kilometres and a change in altitude of three thousand and eighty-five metres, not counting any dips. The best winning time is just under five hours.

We struggled on through the jungle until we went through the tree line. The open savannah above the tree line had been recently burnt and was just black ash and only a few of the larger shrubs' upper limbs had escaped the flames. The gradient also steepened noticeably. At least in the jungle you couldn't see very far ahead, so the scenery was constantly changing. But here on the open savannah part of the trek, you could see the track for a long way, and it was all up.

We reached New Hut in the late morning and had an early lunch. There was another group of six teenagers who were coming down, having spent a night higher up the slope. They looked exhausted, and for a group of teenagers, they were surprisingly quiet.

From the hut, the gradient got steeper again. Our porters met us at the hut as we were having lunch. We were also approached by another trekker who introduced himself as Daniel, with his own guide and porter. He was doing the same three-day route as ourselves, so we would see him several times over the next few days.

When we set off again, we couldn't see where the path led up the mountain, as it was so steep, but, as there were several people on the trail ahead of us, we could see their heads and so where the trail went. Not only was the trail steep, but there were several large steps on the track, which were demanding on the leg muscles

In the early afternoon we could see the roof of Hut Number Two ahead of us. We finally reached the hut to discover that there were several buildings creating a complex, with a sign announcing it as the Fako Mountain Lodge. There were five dormitory buildings, a main building housing a bar and a restaurant, and several chalets scattered about the site. This was much more than we had expected, as we had only been told about the upgrading option from a tent to a chalet.

There were some flat wooden platforms erected up the slope, opposite the main building and our tent was pitched on one of these. We had been told that it would be a six-man tent but in fact it was only a four-man tent. Therefore, it would be cramped and there would be nowhere to put our bags. However, Sarah had planned well, and had several black plastic bin liners into which we could put our rucksacks to protect them from rain, and any morning dew outside the tent.

We spent the afternoon with some drinks and playing the card version of Monopoly. Daniel joined us but he had bought the complete package. His porter also cooked his food for him, so we chatted while he waited for his evening meal. The drinks was expensive; more than three times the price back in the Miramar Hotel, but this wasn't surprising as we were half way up a mountain at two thousand eight hundred and fifty metres.

We cooked our supper ourselves, consisting of some chopped vegetables and noodles. It was here that we discovered that the avocado and the bananas had had such a rough ride up the mountain that they were just mush; not even good enough for guacamole, so we had to throw them away. The porters had cooked their meal and we just added some more fire wood and boiled the water for the noodles. We were above the tree line, but wood is provided, either carried up by the porters or brought up by the bi-weekly 4x4 supply truck that comes up the rough mountain trail to deliver to the huts.

We were all tired, and so we were in bed before it was dark. It would be a six a.m. breakfast and a seven-thirty a.m. start on the trail. I had to get up during the night. I had been awake for ages trying not to think of going to the toilet, and I probably didn't need to go, but the longer you think about it, the more that you must go. But trying to get out of a tent in the dark without waking anyone else was virtually impossible. I tried but failed. As it was, everyone was awake, and tthree of us got up to go to the toilet.

At breakfast, our porters were supposed to clean the pots, the pan and the cutlery, but they were dirty, so we had to wash them with baby wipes and hopefully boiling the water would kill off any residual germs. But the tea did taste a little unusual. The girls had muesli and I had some leftover cold noodles for breakfast.

Daniel had his breakfast cooked for him, and served by his guide, and I was jealous of his cooked full English breakfast. But then I just thought of the difference in price and I consoled myself with the fact that I had saved twenty dollars on every meal.

Daniel set off at seven a.m. and we followed at seven-thirty a.m. carrying our day packs, our water and our lunch. The porters would repack our sleeping bags and other equipment and they would catch up with us later.

It wasn't far in distance terms to the summit, but it was a gruelling one thousand two hundred and forty-five metre vertical ascent over four kilometres. We were soon spread out over the trail, but we regrouped at a volcanic cave. It was a former lava tunnel where the roof had collapsed and there was a short tunnel. The top of the lava had solidified as it pooled in a hollow, but somewhere further down the mountain the lava still flowed, so there was still an outlet and the tunnel formed as the lava continued to escape down the mountain.

We had still more distance upwards to go, with only one break from the relentless strain on the legs, where the terrain was flat, but the wind was still strong and it was in full sun, so while the walking was easier, it was still at altitude and hard work. Just beyond this was Hut Number Three; nothing as sophisticated as the complex at Hut Number Two, as it was just a shed. Daniel was having a break there and Rowan and I had a chance to swap stories about aching legs, whilst we waited for Jacci and Sarah to catch up to us.

Then we had the last five hundred vertical metres to go to reach the summit. The summit of this volcano is unusual as it is not on the rim of the caldera. In fact, there is no major caldera and the summit is made up of multiple fissures and vents with several near the summit, but none are major features.

We walked through a cinder field and it was hard work just like walking through soft sand, so a great strain on the legs. We were nearly at the summit, but since this was Sarah's first volcano, we stopped just short of the peak and we waited for her. Once she reached us and had recovered from the strain of trekking at altitude, we climbed up the last few metres with Sarah leading the way, and we were finally at the summit.

We walked down past several vents and fissures and then through various lava fields. Lava fields are hard work to walk through, as they have multiple drops and peaks to negotiate, something like peat hacks on the Pennine Way.

Then, after a long walk through several lava fields and being both sunburnt and windblown we arrived at the 1982 eruption fissures. The later 2000 eruptions were from the same line of fissures, but a little further down the mountain. They had covered the local area in ash and the walking was hard work.

Then it was down past the line of small vents to the last camp. It had the same architecture and organisation as the previous major campsite. We bought cold beers and played more card Monopoly. Daniel was there and he was relaxing with a beer as we cooked our evening meal of noodles and vegetables. Rowan and I had both booked a shower while our meal was cooking, but I was late getting into the shower. Rowan had used-up all the hot water and I had a cold shower.

The mountain is so high that it creates its own weather, and there was thunder and lightning. It is so high and the storms so regular that it is also called Thunder Mountain. But the height also meant that it was another eight-hour walk to get off the mountain. The first hour was across savannah, with numerous burnt out areas. We crossed a lava field from the most recent 2000 eruption. The rock was only covered by mosses, as other plants had yet to establish themselves.

Just a little further down the track, we crossed a lava field created by the 1982 eruption. There was just a couple of decades difference, but this area of jumbled rocks had mosses plus grasses poking out from between the rocks, but it would be several more decades before the area was fully colonised by the full range of plants found in established areas of the savannah.

Then it was a long trek through jungle down the Guinness path. It was thick damp jungle. We knew that we were getting close to civilisation as there were clearings in the jungle, some recently created, whilst others had had crops planted and these were ready to be harvested. The most popular crop was Elephant Ears, a type of palm whose roots develop a yam like root.

It was here that we found a chameleon. It was walking across the path that we were following and despite our presence, it still walked on at its own leisurely pace. Then we arrived at the village and to a tarmac road and to where Thompson was waiting for us. I tipped the guide and the porters on behalf of the group, and we were driven back to the Miramar Hotel in Limbe.

Our legs were aching, and it was painful to walk anywhere. I had a few blisters, but Sarah had seven. I paid for an upgrade at the hotel, and after a few days walking at altitude and camping, I had a great night's sleep; the first for several nights, but I couldn't have a lie in as we were due to leave at eight a.m.

Next was a drive day, to get from Limbe, through Douala and along the coast to relax at Kribi. We were camping in the grounds of a hotel situated on the beach, next to a small river with golden sandy beaches. You could walk along the beach for two kilometres, to reach another river, where it cascaded across rocks to plunge into the sea.

I walked along the beach and I stopped for a drink at one of the hotels before heading back to my hotel. There were some trinket sellers and one of them had several elephants, so a bought a group of a dozen elephants for my daughter, and it was my opportunity to re-establish the family tradition and create a large herd.

It was time to move on, but the chambermaid who had taken my washing was not due to start work until eight a.m. the same time that we planned to leave. As it was, she didn't turn up for work on time, but I had a little extra time as the truck had to get out of the hotel compound and due to the soft sand, we had to get the sand mats out. However, the chambermaid still didn't appear, so I had to get another member of staff to open the laundry room and I had to sort through piles of washing myself to get my things.

It was a long drive day to get from Kribi to Yaounde, the capital of Cameroon, which was a busy city, with lots of hustle and bustle, cars and people. We were to spend several nights at the Presbyterian Mission on top of a hill, but regrettably, the reception for internet and for phones was poor. The hill is dominated by several large water towers, which can be seen from many parts of the city. There were also several communication masts, more than a dozen; and despite that, the internet and the phone reception was poor. I was obviously on the wrong network.

The site was going to host a wedding the next day, and there were a lot of people putting up tents, setting out tables and chairs, arranging flowers, disco lights and arranging decorations. That was more than I was prepared to accept, so I booked a hotel and then I walked into the city. I searched for a DHL branch, to send my herd of elephant's home, but they wanted a lot of paperwork, receipts, and a certificate of origin and I couldn't find bubble wrap anywhere.

By chance, I found a Tupperware shop with a box just about the right size. I wrapped the elephants in tissue paper and squeezed then into a three D puzzle of interlocking legs and trunks in the box with no space to spare. It took several goes to get them all in, but it worked, and I posted them home from a local post office.

I walked back to the Presbyterian Mission and the wedding in the grounds had finished at four p.m. the day before and was mostly dismantled. Some of the group had gone to see a football match at the local stadium. I assumed that they would arrive back late, inebriated and noisy, so I went to bed.

We left the city and the tarmac and travelled south over jungle tracks to Ambam and onwards to the border.

CHAPTER 16
GABON

We crossed the Ntem River into Gabon. If I was faithful to my plan to follow the West Coast of Africa, I should be crossing into Equatorial Guinea. It is a former Spanish colony and the only country in Africa where the official language is Spanish. The country is largely on the mainland, but its capital, Malabo is on the island of Bioko, off the coast of Cameroon. It was first discovered by Fernando Pó in 1474, and the first colony was established in 1474. The Treaty of El Pardo between Portugal and Spain in 1778 ceded Bioko to Spain, and it became independent in 1968.

The country has extensive oil reserves and has the highest gross domestic product per capita in Africa, but the wealth is very unevenly distributed, and most of the population live in poverty, without access to clean water. Infant mortality for those under five years old is said to be twenty percent. The current president is Teodoro Obiang who has ruled for over three decades. There are elections, but they are considered a sham and there have been a dozen attempted coups. Opposition is ruthlessly crushed and newspapers are censored. The authoritarian government has the worst human rights record in the world, and it is one of the most corrupt places in the world. It didn't seem a nice place to visit. Visas are difficult to get, and the most difficult issue was that the land borders are shut. Therefore, we were bypassing Equatorial Guinea and going straight to Gabon.

Gabon has a link to eighteenth century piracy, in the form of Bartholomew Roberts, also known as Black Bart. He was born John Roberts in Pembrokeshire in Wales in 1682 and he went to sea at the age of thirteen. He was a second mate on the slave ship *Princess*, under captain Abraham Plumb, that anchored off

Anomabu on the Gold Coast, now called Ghana, in 1719. Their ship was captured by pirates led by captain Howell Davis, who was also a Welshman from Pembrokeshire. The crew were forced to join the pirates.

Davis soon discovered Robert's ability as a navigator and often conferred with him, often in Welsh so that their plans would be kept secret from the rest of the crew. Davis was killed in an engagement with the Portuguese in Príncipe, and Roberts was elected as the new captain. From 1719 onwards, he raided ships off the coasts of West Africa, Brazil, the Caribbean and as far north as Newfoundland. He was probably the most successful pirate ever and captured over four hundred vessels. In February 1722, *HMS Swallow* under captain Chaloner Ogle engaged the pirates off the coast of Cape Lopez, just down the coast from Libreville, the current capital. Black Bart was killed by grapeshot and buried at sea, before the pirates surrendered.

Ogle captured two hundred and seventy-two pirates; sixty-five were black and sold into slavery and fifty-two were hanged. Ogle helped himself to some gold in Robert's cabin; he received a knighthood for his naval actions, and eventually became an admiral. Black Bart's death is considered to be the end of the Golden Age of Piracy.

French explorer Pierre Savorgnan de Brazza led his first mission to Gabon in 1875 and the area became a French colony in 1885. It became part of French Equatorial Africa in 1910 and became independent in 1960.

Oil provides the governments revenue and comprises eighty percent of its exports. The next most important extractive industries are manganese mining and timber. There is also some gold production and a large, yet unexploited, iron ore deposit. However, income distribution is unequal and just twenty percent of the population earn over ninety percent of the income.

We weren't going to the capital, Libreville on the coast, but instead we were going to the centre of the country to see Lopé National Park. There was thick lush jungle everywhere as we drove south. Lopé National Park was created in 1946 and has both thick jungle and some of the original savannah created after the last ice age. It is home to a population of elephants, buffalo and the famous African drill monkeys. We heard and saw the monkeys, but we were disappointed that we didn't see any big game.

After a safari through the savannah, we continued south, along dirt roads toward the Republic of Congo. We were promised more bad jungle tracks described as 'challenging road conditions' and despite what the guide book promised, we made good time towards Ndende and we bush camped near the border, so that we could be up early and hopefully be at the front of the queue.

CHAPTER 17
REPUBLIC OF THE CONGO

We were called forward one by one by the immigration official. The others ahead of me had got through successfully but the official in front of me had my passport and my yellow fever certificate, but he was asking for a letter and I didn't have one. It was the letter with the address of the hotel that I was booked into that I had used when applying for my visa in Lomé, Togo some weeks before. Simple, but I didn't have a paper copy. Luckily, I had an electronic version on my laptop, and he seemed satisfied with that.

Then, we had only three hundred and sixty kilometres to go to Pointe-Noire and to a bush camp on the beach. We would be staying at the La Brasserie de la Mer, which is a beachfront restaurant with some spare land behind it, that we were going to camp on. We would be there for several days and after so many days on the road, I wanted an upgrade. Rooms were available opposite the restaurant, but they only had one spare room for one night, but I took it anyway.

I soon found myself very popular with the other members of the group. The camp facilities were rather basic, and I had hot water in the shower, a flushing toilet and air conditioning. I had a queue of people using my room, as I sat at the bar. It was International Women's Day and there were several groups of ladies celebrating at the bar. Many of them were wearing dresses made from the same material, and so you could tell who was from which group. They must have been at the bar for a while before I arrived, as they were raucous and singing, and every now and again there was a burst of laughter or a collective cheer and beer bottles raised to lips.

The next day I moved back to a tent behind the restaurant. We had a few days to relax on the beach and for Gareth to do a few jobs on the truck. Meanwhile, the cook group needed to go into town to do a cook group shop, so I tagged along with them in a taxi to go to a supermarket on the main shopping street.

We took a taxi into the centre of the city and we found a large supermarket. I left the cook group to do the shopping and I walked down the main street. There are several government and other buildings there, built after the First World War, and they are all in the art deco style and well preserved. At the bottom of the main street is the main railway station.

The railway was built between 1921 and 1934 to connect the port to Brazzaville and river navigation further up the Congo to the sea. There are some massive rapids on the river between Brazzaville and the sea, that prevent ships from going up the river, hence the need for the railway to transport goods.

The railway station is an odd mix of alpine and art deco styles. It is a massive building for such an underutilised railway. There are only three trains a week to the capital. The journey takes more than twelve hours overnight, so most people take a plane which takes under an hour. Unlike the other buildings, the fabric of the railway station needs some serious renovation and refurbishment. There are giant holes in the roof and inside, the plaster work and the ornate art deco windows need attention.

On the way back, I checked out the best hotel in the city, the Atlantic Palace Hotel. The reception area was designed in a nineteenth century ornate French style, as were the bar and the restaurant areas. It had a large swimming pool and exquisitely manicured gardens. It was undoubtedly the best hotel in town, but it also had the highest prices. I would have liked an upgrade for a night or two but I couldn't afford even the price for the cheapest room, so I had to return to La Brasserie de la Mer and sleep in a tent on the beach.

Now that I knew the route into the centre of the city, I planned to walk into town early the next morning. I got up and set out at dawn. The security guard at the restaurant was concerned about my safety, and he advised against it, saying that there were many bad people about. I looked up and down the streets and saw no one at such an early hour and whilst late evening may be dangerous, I am not sure that thieves and muggers are early risers. But he was so insistent that I sat down overlooking the beach to watch the sun rise and I waited until it was light.

Mat was up early as well, and eventually we set off to walk together towards the centre. The sun was shining down and warming the morning air rapidly. I was looking for a coffee en route, but only a few shops were open, and none sold coffee. We got as far as a local supermarket that was open, so we had an ice cream each instead of coffee and we bought some ice and bread for breakfast and we returned to the camp.

Back in camp I met Jacob and Mila. They were going south from Holland to Cape Town by motorbike and would be stopping at some of the same places as we were due to stop at, so we would probably meet one another again. They told us that the local Chinese hotel did coffee and that they had internet. I wasted no time and I walked up there and had a small strong black coffee. I wanted milk in my coffee but there was none, so I had to have it black. The hotel was large with several stories and extensions, but I saw few clients whilst I sat and drank my coffee in their café.

After several days on the beach relaxing, departure day arrived, and we said goodbye to Pointe-Noire, to travel about thirty kilometres to the border, to leave the Congo and to crossover into Cabinda. This is part of Angola but it is separated from the rest of the country by a strip of land along the banks of the Congo River that is part of the Democratic Republic of Congo, formerly called Zaire and prior to that, the Belgium Congo. It was only separated from the rest of the country by the river until the Belgium Congo acquired the strip of land on the southern bank of the river under the terms of the Berlin Conference in 1885. There was a lot of horse trading at that conference and a lot of odd borders and straight lines were created, rather than following natural features such as mountain ridges and rivers or traditional tribal areas.

When Portugal finally granted independence, Cabinda was due to be an independent country, but they left so quickly that they took a short cut and coupled it with the main part of their former colony of Angola, so that Cabinda is an enclave and separated from the rest of the country by a slice of the Congo and the Congo River.

There is a small but active independence movement to liberate the area from Angolan control called Front for the Liberation of the Enclave of Cabinda, shortened to FLEC with offices in Paris. They claim that the three former kingdoms that make up Cabinda had a separate agreement to recognise Portuguese control over the area, and therefore they should be a separate and independent country, and that the occupation by Angola is illegal. There are sporadic shootings and demonstrations that can develop into riots. However, independence is a pipe dream, as the area is rich in oil, which provides a huge amount of foreign earnings and revenue for the Angolan government. Therefore, it is unlikely that they will be able to easily become an independent nation; but petrol is cheap and we stopped at a petrol station and filled both the running tank and the reserve tank, for half the price of petrol at home.

We went straight through Cabinda as we didn't feel safe to stop and we covered the hundred and thirty-five kilometres to the Angolan Cabinda/Democratic Republic of Congo border in a single day. We didn't have time to complete all the formalities before the border shut, so we camped at the police barracks on the Angolan side of the border until it opened in the morning.

CHAPTER 18
THE DEMOCRATIC REPUBLIC OF THE CONGO

The border opened and we were first in line to fill in the necessary forms. It took an hour to leave Cabinda, to drive the hundred metres across no man's land and then queue for two hours to be interviewed and photographed for entry into the Democratic Republic of the Congo, often shortened to just DRC. We did the usual things we did at most other borders, such as changing money and buying SIM cards.

Something else was happening as the road was cleared by police and they lined up for inspection. Down the road that led to the border was a convoy of vehicles approaching at speed with their headlights on and flashing blue lights. The border post was being visited by a big wig. The cars screeched to a halt in a cloud of dust and the dignitaries and their body guards got out. There was a film crew recording everything as the lined-up police had an inspection and there were a couple of speeches followed by clapping, and then the officials went inside and the line-up was dismissed.

It was midday when we left the border post and we had passed the last checkpoint. Unlike the road to the border which was tarmac, the road leading away from the border on the DRC side was just sand and gravel. The scenery had changed, and it was largely rolling grassland with just a sprinkling of trees. It was open savannah, but the soil conditions also had an influence. It was loose well-drained sand with thin soil and the trees found it difficult to become established there and hence the open rolling grassland. I was surprised that although there were fields cleared of grass to plant cassava and peanuts, there were large stretches of uninterrupted grass, ideal for grazing but not a single animal to be seen. There were odd shaped fields with a series of ridges in unordered rows. The land is not very fertile and can only grow crops for one or two seasons before it is exhausted, and the field is then abandoned, and another area is cultivated.

This was a very different country from what I had expected as I had thought that it was all jungle. I was very aware of its history and its reputation as a potentially dangerous place. It is the second largest country in Africa after Algeria (the largest country used to be Sudan until Southern Sudan obtained independence in 2011). Most people recognise the country's former names such as Zaire, used from 1971 to 1997 or historically, as the Belgian Congo.

The area was extensively explored by Henry Morton Stanley; the same man who went to Africa to find Dr Livingstone. His trip was funded by King Leopold the Second of Belgium, who obtained formal possession of the area under the terms of the Berlin Conference in 1885. He proceeded to make it his personal property and it was called the Congo Free State from 1885. In 1908 it was annexed by Belgium and it became the Belgian Congo. The indigenous population was used as forced labour, firstly to harvest wild rubber, and later to fulfil ivory quotas and to build infrastructure; and millions died there from overwork and disease.

The country achieved independence in 1960 under Patrice Lumumba. He had insisted on no transitional period and wanted independence straight away. The levers of government were still in the hands of Belgian nationals and there were few educated or experienced Congolese ready to take over their roles. This resulted in the masses of Belgium administrators, civil servants, police and army officers handing over control to people who were untrained and unused to being in positions of responsibility.

The provinces of Katanga and Kasai attempted to secede, and there were various factions seeking control. It was still during the Cold War period, and Lumumba became increasingly erratic in his policy making decisions and he threatened to call in Russian troops to assist him in his attempts to consolidate control of the country. Lumumba was assassinated and after more instability

Mobutu Sese Seko came to power in a coup in 1965 and ruled it as a dictatorial one-party state for the next thirty-two years. His anti-communist stance earned him support from the United States of America, who did little to counter his excesses of embezzlement, patrimony and corruption, whilst he stood against communist aggression. He ruled until he was overthrown in 1997 by Laurent-Désiré Kabila in a coup. The turmoil, civil wars and invasions that the country has suffered partly explains why it is the second poorest country in the world with income per capita of only USD753.

We passed through Muanda, a large town, but the road still did not have any tarmac. The rainy season had not reached this area yet, and it was still parched with evidence of wild fires in burnt out areas. Some distance from the road there were plumes of smoke rising into the blue sky, showing that the undergrowth was still tinder dry. As we passed the fires near the road, we heard the crackling of the fire and were blasted by the heat. The rains when they came would put the fires out, but it would make the already poor roads so muddy as to be impassable. The scenery was open rolling grassland with only the occasional tree. It was very unlike my expectation of jungle.

We stopped on the road where a tree had fallen over, to collect firewood but it was still green; but lying in the grass a little further away from the side of the road was another fallen tree, so we used the chain saw to chop it up and we packed as much as we could into the wood locker.

A man on a motorbike came by and stopped. He showed us a pangolin he had captured. It is a scale covered mammal with a long tail, and it is an endangered species. When threatened it can curl itself up into a ball like a hedgehog. The man was taking it to the market to sell, as its meat is a favoured bush meat and its parts are also used in Chinese medicine, so it is a valuable item for a poor farmer.

Yesterday we covered only forty-five kilometres in an afternoon, but we did stop for lunch and to pick up some wood. Therefore, we were up at dawn for an early start and by midday we had got as far as Boma, giving us seventy-five kilometres for the day, so it was more successful in distance terms than the day before. After Boma, there were tarmac roads again and we made better time.

We drove out beyond the city limits and we started to look for somewhere to stop for lunch, but there was nowhere suitable. Finally, we stopped at two p.m. but no one complained as, it being later in the day, the truck provided some shade from the blistering sun. There was a light breeze to cool us down, and a late lunch meant a shorter afternoon.

We moved into some hills and for the first time in the DRC we saw jungle with mahogany trees, thick stands of bamboo and thick undergrowth. It was also the day that the sun finally passed us overhead. It had been coming north from its apogee on the Tropic of Capricorn. On the 25th of March it would be on the equator, but we had crossed the equator a few days earlier, and the sun was still moving north. The day before I stood in the sun at midday and it was directly overhead. Today, I stood in the sun at midday with a compass in my hand, and there was a slight shadow to the south. From now on the sun would rise in the east and set in the west as usual, but at midday it would be to the north of us. The significance of this is that if you know the time and where the sun is, you can work out the compass points.

That afternoon, we reached Matadi on the banks of the mighty Congo River. We stopped on the bluff overlooking the river, to view the town below on the riverbank and the docks. This is where the only bridge to cross the river lies. This is the largest suspension bridge in Africa at over five hundred and twenty metres long. It was completed in 1983 by a Japanese consortium. It is the only bridge on the Congo River proper. The next bridge is two thousand two hundred kilometres away by road, or three thousand eight hundred kilometres by river, over the Lualaba River; a tributary of the Congo. The river here is eight kilometres below the first rapids upstream, which makes navigation impossible further upstream. The water is turbulent and although it's a port, ships don't want to berth there for long, as the current will pull continuously at their hawsers, so they will want to be underway again as soon as possible.

The Congo is the second longest river in Africa at four thousand seven hundred kilometres after the Nile, and the second largest in the world after the Amazon in terms of discharge. It is also the deepest river in the world with depths of up to two hundred and twenty metres. Its drainage basin is the third largest after the Amazon and the Plate Rivers. It is the only river to cross the equator twice.

Matadi is a major port and, due to the rapids, everything must be transhipped here from ships to rail, to bypass the rapids, to continue the journey upstream to their final destinations. The railway to Kinshasa starts here, to bypass the rapids and it runs for three hundred and sixty-six kilometres.

We were stopping for the night at the Catholic Mission in the centre of the city. It is a seminary, convent and a school for over five hundred pupils and we arrived just as the children were leaving. We made a big hit with a lot of the pupils waving and cheering and shouting; all were happy to see us and to practice some English or French. We were causing some congestion at the main gates until they were opened. Until then, traffic had to squeeze around us and through the crowds of waving children. So, for the safety of the children I was glad when the gates opened, and we entered the seminary. We were directed to one of the courtyards where we put up our tents.

The Mission has several separate school compounds, each dedicated to a different age group. They let us camp overnight, but they asked if we could leave early, so as not to be a distraction for the children. That was fine with us, as we wanted to get to the border early.

We were woken by the choir singing hymns for early morning mass. We put our tents away, and packed away the kitchen, as the first of the school children arrived for their day at school. We had been mobbed on our way in, and we attracted as much attention as we tried to leave. The first school children to arrive crowded at the gates and even once through, there were plenty of children on their way to school in groups, who stopped to wave.

We stopped at a local market on the outskirts of Matadi. Jacci and I were cooking in two night's time and so without any ice to refrigerate the meat, we had to think of a vegetarian meal, subject to what we could find in the market. It was only meant to be a short stop, as we needed to get over some bad roads, and get to the border, but the stop was longer than planned. Sarah had a parasite that she probably collected in Pointe-Noire and she needed to find a pharmacist.

They didn't have the right medication, but they referred her to a doctor. The receptionist understood the urgency and pushed her to the front of the queue. The doctor spoke excellent English, as he had trained in London and he gave Sarah an injection. But despite all their help in speeding up the process, Sarah was over half an hour late.

Meanwhile back at the truck, a local drunk had fallen over in the road, as if hit by the truck, and a crowd was forming, and the police had arrived. We were also a curiosity, and the crowd was stopping traffic from moving, so the police were shouting and waving their guns around, to move the crowd on, to get traffic flowing, and to find out what had happened to the man lying in the road.

The story about the man lying in the road having nothing to do with us was explained to the police, with some help from local eye witnesses, and after handing over a few cigarettes they were appeased, but they told Gareth to move the truck, as they moved the crowd on. We had left Mat at the first parking spot, so that he could direct Sarah to the new parking place, a few hundred metres down the road. It all meant that we were late leaving, and we still had a long way to go over poor roads, and a border to cross.

We set off, only to be stopped by a section of one-way traffic, with the other half of the road closed by a long line of cones, so we were losing more time. We waited whilst traffic built-up, until the lights changed, and we went down the hill, over a bridge and then into hills that turned into mountains.

There were wide vistas of gorgeous scenery, steep slopes covered with grass with a few trees as the road snaked through the mountains. We turned off the main road and we had sixteen kilometres to go over a gravel and sand track to the border.

It took an hour to leave the DRC and then two hours to get into Angola again; so, it was late afternoon by the time we had cleared all the formalities and exchanged some money. We drove out of the small border town of Luva and we found a bush camp next to a stream. It wasn't deep enough to swim, but it gave us an opportunity to cool off, and wash after a long hot day.

CHAPTER 19
ANGOLA

Our first stop in Angola was forty kilometres from the border at Mbanza Kongo, previously the capital of a large African kingdom when the Portuguese arrived. The road was just a rough track until we came to the outskirts of the urban sprawl, and it became a flat smooth tarmac road and then we were in the centre of Mbanza Kongo.

There was the cathedral to see, the burial place of several of their kings, and a museum, which was previously the king's residence. There is also the judgment tree, a large tree from which those who were found guilty of a serious crime were hanged. On a roundabout near the centre of the town is a monument, tactfully worded for all those who gave their lives during the independence struggle. Therefore, it covers the fallen of each side during both the resistance to Portuguese rule and later, the three main belligerents during the internal civil war.

The first trading post in Angola was established by the Portuguese at Soyo at the mouth of the Congo River. Luanda was founded in 1575 and Benguela was fortified in 1587. The colonial settlements were mainly sited along the coast and along navigable rivers. The slave trade was abolished in Angola in 1836, and existing slaves were freed in 1854, but the government found it hard to enforce the law and slave ships continued to leave for Brazil for decades as slavery in Brazil wasn't abolished until the end of the nineteenth century.

Angola's borders were defined by the Berlin Conference in 1885. It was about the same time that expeditions started to penetrate the interior, and more colonists were arriving to settle in the new lands. By 1960 there was a growing nationalist movement for an independent Angola, which was resisted by the government in Lisbon. In 1961, the first shots were fired in a liberation war, that was to last for the next thirteen years.

There was the National Front for the Liberation of Angola (FNLA), led by Roberto Holden, recruited mainly from the Bakongo tribe, from refugees in Zaire, and those located in the north of the country. The National Union for the Total Independence of Angola (UNITA), recruited largely from the Ovimbundu tribe, led by Jonas Savimbi in the centre and southern areas of Angola. The Marxist People's Movement for the Liberation of Angola (MPLA), was largely an Ambundu tribe-dominated organization, led by Agostinho Neto, with a strong following in Luanda, and to the north and the east. All three organisations fought the Portuguese and vied for both local and international support, but the MPLA received the most support from Russia, Cuba and China, plus several non-aligned states.

A revolution in Portugal led to a ceasefire, and independence in 1975, with the three factions initially agreeing to work together, but as Portuguese forces retreated to Portugal, each faction sought to rearm and to occupy strategic locations, and fighting broke out, and the country descended into civil war. Russian arms shipments to the MPLA led to CIA and Zairean support for the FNLA and for UNITA. The MPLA benefited from the arrival of Cuban troops to assist it. This was still during the Cold War and a proxy war was being fought, so Zaire and the United States of America, supported the FNLA, and UNITA received material support from the United States of America and from South Africa.

The FNLA were defeated, but UNITA continued to fight until a ceasefire was agreed and general elections were held but UNITA disputed the results and they returned to the battlefield. A final ceasefire was only achieved when Jonas Savimbi was killed in action in 2002, and UNITA gave up its military wing with its troops being absorbed into the nation's army and national elections were held. However, various amendments to the constitution have reinforced the dominant one-party system and the MPLA are still the dominant political force in the country, with serious doubts about freedom and the exercise of voter's rights with voting lists being out of date, and other flaws in the voting system.

The result of the thirty years of war is that many fled to the cities, which are large and overcrowded, with insufficient infrastructure to support the population. The countryside is littered with mines and of the estimated thirty-seven million mines in Africa, ten million of them are in Angola. There are a lot of both war veterans and innocent civilians who were injured by the mines and are now amputees. Charities such as the HALO Trust do a marvellous job of clearing the mines, but there are still accidental incidences being recorded. The wildlife in the areas of the heaviest fighting has also suffered from troop movements, the battles and hunting for bush meat.

There is tension caused by the unresolved Front for the Liberation of the Enclave of Cabinda (FLEC) insurgency in Cabinda, and although the government receives vast revenues from oil and mining minerals such as diamonds and gold, income distribution in the country is very uneven, and not enough of the government revenues are being spread around the whole population.

We headed west through scenic rolling countryside, towards the coast at Nzeto, where we turned south down the main road which runs parallel to the coast. We turned off, to take a farmer's track to Port Pesqueira for a bush camp on the beach. The truck managed the track well enough, but as it reached the beach it got stuck in the sand. We had to use the sand mats to cross the last stretch, and then we parked the truck on the beach. There was some time to have a swim, but not for Jacci and I whose turn it was to cook the evening meal.

Then, after using the sand mats again to get off the beach, we took the main road into Luanda. After so many gravel tracks and jungle and passing through poor rural areas and around thatched huts, the urban sprawl of Luanda had dual carriageways, flyovers, traffic jams and multi-storey modern buildings. The cars were clean and modern, the lights worked, and they were no old rusty battered hulks. Despite the number of tall modern concrete buildings housing offices, hotels and residential apartments, plus all the new developments being built, accommodation is in short supply and very expensive as are the prices in the shops. We stopped to do some shopping and were horrified at the prices.

Meanwhile, Sarah went to a private hospital as her parasitic worm was still moving and the previous injection had not been successful. The doctor gave her a prescription, but then there was a problem trying to find a pharmacist who stocked the right medicine. A stranger at the pharmacy was having problems finding the right medicine for his mother but he offered to drive Sarah to a large pharmacy which would satisfy them both. He was very generous and he drove her back across the city to re-join the truck.

The city was too expensive for us, so we drove forty kilometres down the coast to bush camp at Miradouro da Lua, the Moon Valley Viewpoint. There are some rock formations on coastal cliffs there, with sharp pinnacles and deep gullies caused by wind and rain erosion of the soft sandstone. The rocks have several different colours, and the setting sun sets off a blaze of different reds, oranges, yellows and browns.

The last few nights had been so hot that I was sleeping in the pop-up mosquito tent. However, at the viewpoint, thick clouds blew over from the west and it rained in the night. The pop-up only has a fine mesh, which allows a breeze through, and keeps the mosquitoes out, but it is useless against rain.

I was becoming wet, so I put everything that was inside the pop-up under the truck, and I crawled into my sleeping bag, being careful not to bump my head on the axle. I surprised a few of the other early risers as I emerged from under the truck the next morning including one girl who thought that she was alone, being the first one about and she had a quick pee behind the tuck, just inches from me.

On our way back through the centre of the city, we stopped at the old Slave Trading Post to visit the museum. There were some exhibits and artefacts but although the descriptions were all in Portuguese, it was still interesting. From here, the slaves would be walked down to the shore and loaded onto slave ships. The Slave Coast in West Africa was renowned for slaves, but it is estimated that more than five million slaves were shipped to the Americas from Angola, and half of them went to work in the mines or in rubber and sugar plantations of Brazil.

We said goodbye to Mike and Rowan, who were leaving us. Rowan was leaving Africa to visit family in Abu Dhabi, and then she had to start her new job a little earlier than expected. Mike was flying directly to South Africa, to tour around the country by car.

We drove east from Luanda and were soon back in rolling countryside covered in jungle. As we left the urban metropolis, we left the modern, vibrant and sophisticated city, and we started to see more of the Africa that I had seen over the last few months. There was more rural poverty, people dressed in rags, mud huts and no water or electricity. Further away from the city there were fewer and fewer farms. There were occasional fields of cassava or groups of banana trees and then fewer and fewer fields until it was just jungle.

There was the occasional village set back from the road. Some of the locals were selling bush meat. We passed one little village where there were dead monkeys hanging from poles by their tails being offered for sale. For poor rural villagers with a deficiency of protein, this is not considered exceptional, although it may be offensive to tourists. They either sell it and use the money for food or eat it themselves. So, wildlife is struggling to thrive even after the end of the civil war, and they still run the risk of setting off some of the millions of land mines left after the conflict.

We stopped at the Shoprite supermarket in a small regional town. There was a railway next to us, and I waited to see a train, but none came through during the hour that I was there. Since it was Saint Patrick's Day, we opened some bottles of beer and we started a party in the back of the truck as we drove. We followed a good road until we crossed a river and the railway, and we were diverted off the road onto a track.

The original line of the road was a construction site, as the road was being upgraded and it will be a great road when it's finished but right now it was back to dirt track and a maximum speed of twenty kilometres per hour. That night at the bush camp in a quarry, Gavin and Elle played some of their collection of Irish music on their iPod, to celebrate Saint Patrick's Day.

We were on our way to visit the Kalandula Falls on the Lucala River, which are the largest waterfalls in Angola, and the third largest in Africa near the town of the same name. They are a hundred and five metres high and four hundred metres wide. There is a look out on the very edge of the cliff, overlooking the gorge and the waterfall, to watch the water plunge over the edge and down into the gorge.

I knew that there was a path down to the bottom of the gorge, so that you can look up at the falls, but all the paths into the jungle near the visitor centre were dead ends. I found it eventually, but it was back up the road and across some fields, but I had time and I wanted the exercise as well as the view. I had been warned that it was muddy but luckily it wasn't too bad, so I was able to get right down to the water's edge. Using some large boulders as stepping stones, I nimbly walked out into the centre of the river, to get the best view of the water falling into the plunge pool, at the base of the falls.

We passed through the towns of Malanje and Cacuso, as we headed towards Piedro Negro. This is a unique formation of rocks rising from the surrounding lower plains. These are harder rocks than the surrounding ones, and are conglomerates, a rock made up of fragments of other rocks and stuck together by minerals in the circulating ground water.

The road leads up to a flat area in the centre of the rocks. This was a former Portuguese military post. There is a police station, a few houses and it's now used as a picnic area and camp site. There is a path that leads up to the top of the rocks from which there are views across the surrounding countryside, and other tall rocks pointing out of the plains.

I walked down the road, back the way we had come, to a place where it is alleged that there are the footprints left by a princess, who was discovered by soldiers as she washed in a stream, and the footprints were created as she ran away. With a bit of imagination, one can discern some footprint size shallow scuffs in the rocks. It was late in the afternoon and no one was about, so I stripped off and I had a wash in the stream.

We camped beside the basketball court of the school that was built here in 2007 but it had been abandoned and was standing empty. There were toilets on site, but we had to carry our own water to them. They were clean but they needed repair. There were school benches and desks in the classrooms, but the corrugated iron roof was peeling off, due to strong winds in the area and there were birds nesting in the rafters. It was a scenic place, but it was a long way from the local villages and while the intention of providing a school was a good idea, no one had consulted the locals, and it had been built in the wrong place, so it was now not used.

It was cold in the morning, but we were at an elevation of one thousand one hundred and forty-five metres. I had to get up during the night to put on a fleece, as it had been so cold overnight. It was cloudy and cool as we drove out of Piedro Negro, and back the way we had come, over the Rio Culava and through Cusoca.

It was to be a drive day and we would be driving all day. The clouds grew thicker and it started to rain. Therefore, we stopped and put a side down so that we wouldn't get too wet. However, the wind changed direction and we had to stop again and put the other side down. It can get very stuffy in the back of the truck without any wind, and with a lot of people. As soon as the rain stopped, we stopped the truck and put the sides up again. Some people also used the stop as a pee stop, so we were stationary for longer than anticipated.

We drove south towards Lumbango near the coast, but it would take a couple of days, so we stopped at a roadside café next to a police checkpoint for the evening. They also had cabins and rooms available stretching up the hill behind the café, plus a swimming pool, but, like many things in Africa, it was broken and only had green rainwater in the bottom. They had a generator that hummed all night which provided power for the café and the street lights around their grounds. We were shown a spot at the far end, where there was some grass and a flat area on the gravel road for the truck.

It had rained during the afternoon and we had just put up the main awning over the kitchen and our tents, when it started raining heavily again. This was not a drizzle nor the normal rain that we get back home, but rather a continuous heavy rainfall of the type that you would expect in a monsoon.

Water was cascading down the gravel track and under the awning and the truck. We used the shovel to build small berms to divert the water away from our kitchen area. The rain was relentless, heavy, but equally short lived as the wind blew it away and we were able to cook a meal under an awning without having our feet standing in a river. I went to the bar where the beer was cold and cheap. Plus, there were electric sockets so that I could recharge my laptop.

We passed more typical African villages with round mud brick huts with thatched roofs, goats foraging in the streets, children playing in the dirt, women washing clothes in dirty water, carrying loads on their heads or working in the fields while the men sat under a tree. Nearing the town of Aleida Nova was the first large scale farming enterprise that I had seen in Angola. There were large fields, some planted with vines, others with a plant that I couldn't identify as we shot past. There were tractors working in the fields, and row upon row of greenhouses but with opaque plastic sides so it was not possible to see what they were growing inside.

There seemed to be fewer road blocks on the rolling savannah, with hills in the distance. There were CRCC signs and depots all along the road. This was the China Road Construction Company, who were upgrading the roads and the upgrade was nearing completion. But whilst they were working on the roads, traffic was being diverted onto temporary rough dirt tracks beside the road. Better roads improve communications, road haulage and the movement of goods. Bus timetables can be revised to give quicker journeys, but it also makes it easier for the rural population to drift to the cities in search of jobs, money and a new life.

In Aleida Nova itself were several brand new, well-appointed and maintained hotels, one with a spa, one with a casino, and another with cabins to rent as well as rooms. Plus, a factory in good condition. It is as often what you don't see as to what you do see. Around here there had been some recent investment and some large agrochemical operation was making use of the weather, the water and the land to grow something which was unusual when agriculture is largely subsistence farming, most things are imported, and the economy is still suffering from decades of warfare.

On the far side of the city was another large commercial farm, this one grew maize in a field that was several kilometres long, beside the road, plus some recently built farm buildings. Most of the agriculture that I had seen to date was subsistence farming, with small fields and perhaps a woman with a small pile of vegetables for sale, sitting at the side of the road.

There were also stands of pine and eucalyptus trees in neat rows, so this was my first sight of any forestry activity, another first and notably using some of the land to be productive. The road goes through some pretty countryside, rolling savannah and dramatic hills and it was a great scenic journey. There were few villages but at a junction of two roads, there was a collection of traders, with temporary stands or with just their wares spread out on blankets or in baskets, in an impromptu market.

That night, we camped under some electric cables held high above us, by soaring pylons. It was a memorable bush camp, as there was a huge storm with thunder and lightning. There was such a downpour that the water was running down the slope and ponding at the bottom, so my tent was partially submerged. I got up, I undid the tent pegs and I dragged my tent up the slight slope.

We drove into Huambo, the provincial capital and Angola's second largest city. The city was founded in 1912 and grew rapidly in economic importance when it became a hub on the Benguela Railway. This was completed in 1929 by Sir Robert Williams who discovered the vast copper deposits in Katanga, now incorporated into the Democratic Republic of Congo. This railway follows the most direct route from the mines to a good seaport on the Atlantic coast to export copper. It was called Nova Lisboa from 1928 until independence in 1975.

We didn't stop in the city, but we parked next to a large supermarket in the suburbs. Jacci and I went cook group shopping, but we went over budget, but I put some extra money into the kitty so that the vegetarians could have some mushrooms for a change.

We arrived in Lubango in the rain. The city was founded in 1885 by a thousand settlers from Madeira who arrived in 1882. We were going to visit Cristo Rei, which is a statue of Jesus which overlooks the town, rather like Christ the Redeemer overlooks Rio, although this statue is not so grand. We passed the Caspar Lodge, a posh hotel and some ethnic rustic cabins for rent on the road up to the statue. There was low cloud and the view was obscured. We had a picnic lunch on the truck hoping that the clouds would blow over, but they obstinately stayed put and we couldn't wait for ever, so we continued to another well-known tourist site for which Lubango is known, the Fenda do Tundavala. This is a cleft in the steep cliff face on one side of the town. There is a kilometre drop down to the valley below, but as with the statue of Jesus, the low cloud cover obscured the view, and all that could be seen from the lookout point was just a sea of fog below us.

We returned to a campsite which was near the top, at an elevation of one thousand eight hundred metres. It was still raining heavily, and we put up the awning so that Noodles and Elle could cook. The forecast was for more cloud, but we camped near the top of the mountain with the hope of the clouds blowing over by the morning. We put our tents up in the rain and I made a few unwelcome discoveries. My Salomon walking boots were not waterproof, I broke the zip on my waterproof jacket and I found a tear in my waterproof trousers, so despite having the right gear, it wasn't doing the job and I was getting wet.

In the morning, there was still cloud but it had stopped raining, and the cloud base was a lot higher than the day before. This time, we saw the cleft and a long way below us was the valley floor. From the lookout point, it is a sheer drop to the valley floor. According to the guide, it takes fourteen seconds for a stone to fall that far, before hitting the bottom, but we took that on trust.

We drove back to Lubango to take the road south. With the better visibility we saw more of the town, which is surrounded on three sides by high cliffs. Set halfway up one of the slopes near the town were some ugly buildings made worse by their bright colours. One was yellow and there were three identical buildings in a bright shade of pink, all of which dominated the skyline.

Angola is still recovering from three decades of war. There is a problem with the landmines and the worst affected provinces are those in the south. There were nineteen thousand Cuban troops in the area, assisting the MPLA. UNITA fought through this area. The Namibian South West Africa Peoples Organisation's military wing had bases here, from which they launched operations over the border in Namibia, then controlled by South Africa. The South African army invaded this area to attack SWAPO bases and to support UNITA in their fight against the MPLA and they shelled Lubango. There are still the remains of the tanks that litter the side of the road. Outside of the capital and outside large towns such as Lubango, there are still poor rural villages that lack power, water supplies and jobs. It looks like much of rural West Africa despite the wealth generated by the oil and mining industries. And then we arrived at the border.

CHAPTER 20
NAMIBIA

We were through the border in record time and consequently, we had some unexpected extra time. We were heading for Etosha National Park and we could either have a long drive day and an extra night in the park or stop early for a bush camp. We unanimously opted for an extra night in the park. We stopped in the border town of Oshikango for lunch and to do shopping.

Everything was such a contrast. The buildings were finished as the architect intended without steel reinforcing bars sticking out of the top and no missing windows or broken doors. The roads were smooth and there were no potholes. There were pavements, gutters and drains. The cars were modern, clean, almost sparkling with good paint work, waxed and shiny and with no dents or bits missing. The people were used to seeing whites and they smiled as they passed us but they didn't stare. As we passed through villages in West Africa, the children had waved at us or had even run after the truck but now they ignored us. But there were also no beggars, and people were better dressed, in clothes without holes and wearing shoes.

There was power and internet connectivity. There were road signs, road names and lamp posts which we had only seen in the larger cities. There were functioning and busy malls. There were illuminated signs instead of just a board with hand written letters daubed in paint. Everything worked as intended and there were no slums, no road side shacks or groups of women selling a few vegetables at the side of the road. How strange that I had become used to all that without realising it. And we were no longer a curiosity.

Namibia was discovered by Portuguese navigators such as Diego Cam in 1485 and Bartolomeu Dias in 1486 but the area was not claimed or colonised by them. Walvis Bay, a large natural deep-water harbour was occupied by the Cape Colony in 1879 and later it became part of South Africa. But the rest of present-day Namibia was largely desert or savannah, and only thinly populated by indigenous tribes. There were some Boer settlers who were escaping from British rule in South Africa and some German and Swedish settlers. During the scramble for Africa, Otto von Bismarck, the German Chancellor claimed the area, and it became a German colony in 1884 and was known as German South West Africa.

The Germans ruled the area with brute force and subjected the indigenous people to dispossession, discrimination and forced labour. The Herero and Namaqua tribes rebelled, and they were brutally repressed by the Schutztruppe, the German colonial army, during the period 1904 to 1907. This is said to be the first genocide in modern history with between fifty per cent and eighty percent of the indigenous tribes killed.

The Schutztruppe never numbered more than two thousand, but when The First World War broke out in 1914, the Germans attacked Walvis Bay and they clashed with Portuguese troops along the border with Angola; although Germany did not declare war on Portugal until March 1916 after the Portuguese had seized several German ships in Lisbon harbour. South Africa had to first consolidate its control of its own territory as it had been only twelve years since the end of the Second Boer War, and there was still some Boer pro-German support, resulting in the Maritz rebellion that had to be contained first. It took allied troops moving up from South Africa a year to capture Windhoek in May 1915, and they only finally defeated the Germans after the Battle of Otavi in July 1915.

South Africa occupied Namibia under a League of Nations mandate, but after the Second World War when former colonies gained independence, South Africa consolidated its hold over Namibia. The South West Africa People's Organisation (SWAPO) created an armed wing in 1966, to fight for independence, which became the People's Liberation Army of Namibia (PLAN), with support from Russia, Cuba and Angola. Fighting continued until a cease fire was agreed in 1989 and independence was achieved in 1990. The economy today is very strong with tourism, agriculture and mining being the major industries. Mining produces more than twelve percent of the GDP and diamond mining produces seven percent by itself.

Looking at a map of Namibia, you will notice a panhandle stretching for over four hundred and fifty kilometres to the north east of the country. This is called the Caprivi Strip. It was named after German Chancellor Leo von Caprivi, who negotiated its acquisition from the United Kingdom in 1890. The intention was to give the German colony access to the Zambesi, and hopefully to the Indian Ocean and its other colony in East Africa, Tankanyika; but nobody had checked the maps or any of the explorer's reports as the Zambesi which flows to the ocean, is unnavigable due to the Victoria Falls. Great Britain agreed to the transfer under the Heligoland-Zanzibar Treaty of 1890, in which Germany gave up its interest in Zanzibar, in return for the Caprivi Strip and the island of Heligoland in the North Sea.

We arrived at the entrance gate to the Etosha National Park in mid-afternoon and we paid our entrance fees. We were in plenty of time to reach our campsite within the specified time. No one is allowed to drive in the park between sunset and sunrise, so everyone had to either exit the park or they had to drive through the gates of their chosen pre-booked campsite before sunset. The sanctions are heavy fines, confiscation of vehicles or the cancellation of bookings and ejection from the park.

We reached our camp at Namutoni, but we would be stopping for just one night, as we were moving on to our scheduled booked site at Halali. The campsite catered for all budgets with up market air-conditioned lodges, and suites for the well-heeled, to rooms to campsites. Within just a couple of hours of entering the park we had seen oryx, elephants, giraffes, hartebeest, wildebeest, several lizards, a leopard tortoise and a dozen different species of birds, plus a couple of black rhinos. We had had a great view from the truck as we were so much higher than people in their cars. Part of the roof just behind the cab, known as the beach, is hinged and can be opened and people can sit up there and get an uninterrupted view across the landscape.

Each campsite is located near a watering hole, which is lit at night and there are viewing platforms behind fences, so although guests are confined to the campsite, there is an opportunity to see the wildlife. I walked to the watering hole but saw little of interest. These are essential for most animals due to the arid nature of the environment but, as the rainy season had started, there was plenty of water in springs and in mud holes, and the vegetation was greener, so the animals didn't need to congregate at the water holes, but there were still some animals to see.

The campsite was extensive, and it catered for different budgets, but there were far more five-star elderly tourists and middle-income cabin hirers than campers. It made me feel that I was a second-class citizen since some of the people at the bar, the café and in the restaurant were wearing brand new best quality linen safari suits and safari hats bought for their holiday that might never be worn again.

We were up early for a dawn safari and we were first in the queue, waiting at the gate for it to be opened. We were going for a drive around the reserve, past several watering holes to see what wildlife was about. We drove along the shore of the Etosha Pan and through the savannah, sometimes open savannah and sometimes open stretches of grass. We saw giraffes, elephants, mongoose, impala, ostriches, eland, zebras, dik diks and plenty of birds, including the secretary bird, one of my favourites, with its most peculiar gait, like a secretary typing, hence the name.

We returned to the camp to take down our tents. We had some time before we were due to leave for our next camp. I went to visit the fort. In the centre of the camp is a large square fort with high walls painted white. It was built in 1906 by the Germans to house a garrison and to control traffic along the road, which used to pass through here. The main road has since been diverted around the edge of the park. The fort was destroyed during an uprising against the German colonial authorities who brutally repressed local rebelling tribes. It was rebuilt so it is a replica of the original fort.

We had a leisurely drive to Halali, our next camp. We saw more eland and giraffes with their odd way of spreading their front legs to reach the water. There was one sitting down with its legs splayed in front of it, and we waited for a while as I wanted to see how it gets up, but it didn't oblige before we had to move on.

One afternoon, we were having a sunset safari in a different part of the park and had driven around, but had not seen much wildlife, as some animals keep still in the mid to late afternoon until the temperature falls, and then they become more active. There were impala, lots of birds, plovers, steenboks, dik diks and we saw a spotted jackal. On our way back to the campsite before the curfew, we saw another jackal. It was limping as it had had an accident, and as they are scavengers, it was probably an encounter with a larger animal that was injured but not yet dead and could still resist. Then we saw another jackal, but it was getting close to curfew, so we didn't linger.

We then saw two black rhinos and we stopped. They were near the road and they didn't wander off into the bush and disappear out of sight like our first sighting on our first day. We took photos as fast as we could, as we were conscious of the time. Gareth drove as fast as he could to get back in time. We saw a white rhino, but we resisted the temptation to call for a stop. It started to rain, and usually we would stop and put the sides down and put the roof back on the beach. But this time, we just carried on and Noodles, Imbi and Chris scrambled back down from the beach to get out of the rain.

We got back to the camp gates with just four minutes to spare; but the drama wasn't over yet. It had rained at the campsite and we had put up the tents when we had arrived, but as it was such a hot afternoon with blue skies, we had left the flysheets off and had rolled up the windows. The rain had come through the mesh of the windows and the inside of our tents were wet. Gareth and Kim had had the sense to put their flysheet on but no one else had.

I used a tee-shirt to mop up the water and then I went to the showers. There was no electricity, so it was gloomy inside, but I had enough light to see what I was doing. Then I had a shower and I rinsed out my tee-shirt, that I had just used to dry the tent inside. The water started out hot but it soon ran cold, and so I had a cold shower.

There were honey badgers in the area, and we had to ensure that all the food was locked away on the truck. They are a menace and they have an aggressive attitude and they have learnt to scavenge around the camp. They tip up rubbish bins and rummage in the contents. They will bite through canvas to get at food. There were reports of them in the camp, but they had come through while we were away and as instructed, none of us had any food in our tents so they had left us alone.

And then the wind picked up and strengthened. In the early evening it rained, a torrential tropical rain, and we had to move the kitchen area. The fire was put out by the rain, so we got the gas cooker out. Luckily the campsite has some areas for cooking and shelter from the rain, so we huddled in the shelter and cooked there until the rain passed.

However, the drainage was not ideal and it pooled around the foundations of the shelter. There was a gutter, but it did little to take the water away, it just took water from the upper areas and deposited it in front of the shelter. It was soon ankle deep and the chefs had to cook with their feet under water.

We ate our evening meal on the truck; the first time that this had happened on the trip. Before our evening meal was served, the wind had picked up so much that it had caught Mikkel's flysheet and it had acted like a sail, and it had pulled the rest of the tent over. The tent and its contents were lying in a puddle. When we told Mikkel about it, he naturally didn't believe us as he thought we were pulling his leg, but when he looked, he had to venture into the rain and right his tent and rescue its contents. His sleeping bag was soaked but luckily it was a warm night and he could sleep without his sleeping bag, and he had dry clothes on the truck.

Whilst we were eating our evening meal, the rain eased off and had stopped by the time we had finished, so we walked to the local watering hole viewpoint, which is on a hill within the compound, overlooking the watering hole which is floodlit, so that gives a great view.

There had been a hyena there earlier in the evening, but there was no activity now, partly as it had rained and there was plenty of water in the leaves and in the puddles, so the animals didn't need to make the possibly dangerous journey to the watering hole.

When the fly sheet is on the tent, it restricts air movement, so it can get stuffy inside the tent. Therefore I often leave it off. Sometimes if the weather looks changeable, I might put the flysheet partially on, and leave the two sides folded back, in order to let some air through.

I had camped under a tree, and during the early morning, the wind had picked up and it shook the tree, and a flurry of water droplets from the branches cascaded onto my tent. I was instantly awake and waiting to hear whether there was likely to be another rain shower. There were a few more drops but there was no rain, but I was awake.

I heard the restaurant staff more than fifty metres away, moving chairs and tables around to set up for breakfast, which was advertised as being available from six a.m. The chair legs scraped on the floor tiles, and as the tables were pushed across the tiles, they made high pitched screeching noises. I was not able to get back to sleep. Kim would be getting some breakfast things ready, just before dawn so we could have a hot drink and make sandwiches for a breakfast on the truck, as we headed out for an early morning safari.

We were due for breakfast at six a.m. for a six thirty a.m. departure, to have a safari drive and then to leave the park and find a bush camp. I heard Kim's alarm go off. I got up and helped with the setting up and then I packed away my tent. We were on the truck, in front of the locked gates, waiting for them to open at six forty-five a.m. The staff were late unlocking the gate, and Gareth had to go and find a member of staff to unlock them. Our first stop was at a watering hole, and sitting there watching the sunrise, downwind of the waterhole, was a young male lion. We stopped some way short of him, perhaps fifty metres away. He was unconcerned about our presence and he continued to lie there, and just occasionally he lifted his head to look around.

He didn't seem to mind us, so Gareth switched on the engine and inched a little nearer. The lion was still unconcerned, and we moved a little further forward. We were within ten metres of him and had a grandstand view. He eventually got up and he sniffed around a fallen tree and moved off thirty metres and lay down watching the waterhole with his back to us.

I had now seen four out of the Big Five with just a leopard to go. We took all the photos that we wanted and then we moved on. Unlike over the weekend, we saw very few vehicles on the roads; and after a few days on safari, and seeing so much wildlife, we were getting blasé about sightings and sometimes we didn't even stop to look at giraffes, jackals or kudu.

There are several different habitats and going further south, some of it was open grassland with little to see. But at one point ahead of us were several vehicles parked at the side of the road with people all looking in one direction. There were three lions, two mature males and an adolescent male lying in some shrubs. They did very little but lie with the occasional lifting of the head. After seeing our young male for more than an hour by ourselves, this wasn't nearly so interesting, so we soon moved on.

We stopped at Okaukuejo Camp for a break. A tall stone tower dominates the entrance, built by the Germans as a lookout point. Guests can walk to the top which is about four storeys high and it gives a view out beyond the camp fence.

Then we left the park via Anderson's Gate and we stopped in Outjo for some shopping. There were dark clouds overhead and some lightning but no rain, but it foreshadowed some bad weather ahead.

We set off and drove away from the weather and then via Khorixas into Damaraland and The Stony Desert. The road changed from tarmac to gravel, and the scenery changed from savannah to just a few shrubs struggling to grow in barren rocky ground devoid of any undergrowth. We passed through some hills and then came to an open area with sand and a few stones, with hills in the distance.

We stopped for a bush camp. The first place that we tried was unsuitable as it was too far from the dirt track, and if it rained heavily, we would take forever to use the sand mats to get back to the rocky but stable gravel track. We moved on and we set up camp just a short distance from the trail, in some low hills. All the time, we could see the dark clouds on the northern horizon, and we heard a lot of thunder and, if you happened to be looking in the right direction, there was a lot of lightning; fork, dagger and sheet.

Luckily it didn't rain during the night, but it hadn't rained for four months. It was a late start after having had several early morning starts for dawn safaris. We had breakfast at eight a.m. and were scheduled to leave at nine a.m. I was up early as usual, and rather than setting up breakfast or taking down my tent, thus making a noise and waking people up, I went for a walk. I walked in the sun's direction to see the sunrise but it was blinding, so I turned around, and I headed in the opposite direction.

I climbed a hill, but it was hard work to see where I was putting my feet and to avoid the needle-sharp thorns that tear at clothes and skin. I returned to the much easier option of walking along the road in the opposite direction to the rising sun. Even here in the stony desert there was life, but I only saw a fox running away from me.

We set off and we took the road to the Petrified Forest for a tour. Our guide Gabriel took us to see some Welwitschia. The plant has two leaves and the plants are male or female. They can grow at one centimetre a month but they can also live for two thousand years and are the national plant of Namibia. He also showed us the euphoria plant which is poisonous. It is used to cover the arrow points with poison, but it is poisonous even when it is dead. The local Damara people never touch it. Even if it is used for firewood, the poison can enter the food and there have been instances of people dying after using the wood for fuel.

In the Petrified Forest there were huge logs one and a half metres in diameter and forty metres long, that had been washed down from present day central Africa two hundred and sixty million to two hundred and eighty million years ago and had since been turned to rock. The trees that we were looking at are between a hundred and twenty and a hundred and sixty years old. Gabriel also pointed out the perfume tree, which the locals used to make themselves smell good. After the Petrified Forest, we went to see the Twyfelfontein rock carvings that are popular with tourists and that hosts several coach loads of tourists every day. It was far too commercial for me and whilst it was interesting, I soon tired of my loud, lazy and ignorant fellow tourists from their five star hotels on a coach trip from the capital complaining about the heat and the dust. They were here to say that they had seen all the top sites in Namibia on a ten day vacation. I was only too happy to retreat to the truck.

Led by a local guide, who introduced himself as Somol, we moved on to the Damara Cultural Museum to see how the locals live.

They were all dressed traditionally, with goat hides around their waists and the children were running around naked and the women had bare chests. The guide took us to visit the pharmacy with the grandmother of the family, explaining the different plants and what they were used for. She spoke in her native language and the guide translated. It was fascinating to listen to her, as she spoke a bushman language which has a series of sounds such as clicks, or a sound made by sucking through your teeth and there are more than three dozen different clicks.

There were ostrich eggs which just one provided enough scrambled eggs for a family and after being blown, the egg shell can be used as a drinking receptacle and the egg can be used to soothe stomach aches. She showed me a stinky poo plant, which can also be used to settle upset stomachs, so called as it produces air as burps and farts, as a side effect. Another plant was used for making tea to relieve stomach cramps. There was another plant to cure earache. The perfume tree is used to make Damara perfume, a shrub with an aromatic smell. There was some red ochre for cosmetics, which is also used to protect against mosquitoes.

The next hut was the bakery. We were told how they collected grass seeds after the rainy season when the grasses have all flowered and formed seeds. The seeds are crushed into a meal, winnowed to remove husks, and then it is used as flour, to make bread.

Then it was on to the brewery. The ingredients were the same grass seeds used for baking, plus honey and water. The mixture was crushed and mixed and then left to ferment to produce a beer. It smelt sweet and it had the familiar smell of beer. It is typically drunk after the men have returned from a hunting trip in the desert.

Then we had a demonstration of a fun African game, owela, which is known in several cultures throughout Africa, but it has several names, and the rules differ in different communities. This version has hollows on a board or in rock measuring four by twelve. The two players sit opposite one another, and each hollow in the first line and half of the second line starts with two pebbles or malara seeds in each. The players then take it in turns to pick up some pebbles and move along the line to capture the other player's pebbles. Play continues until a player has lost all his pebbles. With so many options, a single game can take several days. Disputes between chiefs were sometimes resolved in this way, with the winning player winning the dispute.

The next stop on our tour was an explanation of how they process the hides after an animal has been slaughtered. We had a demonstration of how the hide was stripped of meat and fat on one side, and how the hair was stripped off the other side to create leather. Nothing is wasted and the scraped off hair was used to make blankets.

They also make beads and they thread them onto string which are made from some of the grasses that abound here in the rainy season. They use seeds for beads and the shells of ostrich eggs, which they round off on coarse stones and drill a hole through the centre. They obtain some of the more colourful beads by trading with neighbouring tribes and the bracelets and the necklaces can be quite ornate.

There was also a demonstration of the blacksmiths art. There is iron ore in the hills and the Bushmen would build a fire within an oven to smelt the ore into iron. However, nowadays, they take an easier route and they buy basic metal rods or flats from the town to manufacture whatever they need. These are heated and beaten into weapons such as a spear or a large blade for hunting, or a small blade for kitchen use.

We had a fire lighting demonstration. This consisted of a piece of hard wood with a dimple in the centre and a long thin stick of the same hard wood. A little sand is added to the hole and you then put your hands together and rub to rotate the stick with its end in the hole. The sand acts as resistance and the action of turning the end of the stick in the hole against the sand creates heat.

The other ingredients required for a successful fire lighting were dried donkey dung and elephant dung. Donkey dung is well processed, and fine so it can catch a spark easily. The elephant dung is coarser, but the clearly visible stalks can catch alight from the donkey poo embers. Then you just need some kindling or small twigs and the fire is alight.

Making fire is a very important feat and the children learn how to make fire at the age of seven. Males are unable to marry until they can prove that they can make fire quickly and easily every time.

The tour of the traditional village ended with some singing and dancing and then we exited via the shop so that we could buy some of the things that they had created and amongst our purchases was a fire making set, and we asked for some dried donkey and elephant dung so that we had everything that we would need to light a fire that evening.

Then we went to see the Organ Pipes, a columnar basalt formation. It was interesting if it was your first sighting of such a formation, but not nearly as good as the Giants Causeway or some of the formations in Iceland. A little further up the road is the Burnt Mountain, a magma intrusion under slate, which has metamorphosed and is more resistant to erosion than the surrounding rock, and so has survived.

We went through desert mountain scenery to find a bush camp near the entrance to the Skeleton Coast National Park. En route, we stopped to watch a troupe of baboons walking along, not far from the road.

We set up camp and the kitchen, and then we tried making a fire with the fire making set and it took ages all for nothing. I was cooking with Jacci that evening, so I had to give up trying to use the traditional method and started cooking ove a fire lit with matches. Others tried the traditional method, but no one was successful. Somol our guide and his brother had made it look so easy with just four or five rubs of the stick, but it was obviously a skill that we had yet to acquire.

There was a rustling behind my tent during the night. It was moving slowly and rummaging in the leaf litter and twigs under the tree. I zipped up the tent which I had left open for air. I made some noise and it went quiet, but after a while there was more rustling, and I spent most of the night awake expecting to be attacked. I was luckier than Jacci. We were both up early to pack our tents away and then get breakfast ready for the group. But as she was packing away in the gloom of dawn, she found a snake under her tent which gave her a fright. It was a plastic snake that Mikkel had slipped under her tent the night before which frightened her but gave immense merriment to Mikkel.

CHAPTER 21
THE SKELETON COAST

We entered the Skeleton Coast National Park. Soon after going in, the air temperature dropped noticeably. Just off shore the Benguela current flows north from the Antarctic and cools the air above it and when this moist cool air meets the dry warm air of the desert, it creates thick fog that drifts inland.

It is called the Skeleton Coast due to the large numbers of shipwrecks there. Should the sailors be lucky enough to be washed ashore uninjured, there is nothing for hundreds of kilometres, so most likely they would die of thirst. One shipwreck was a drilling rig that was washed up on the beach, with a collapsed derrick, formerly owned by IDECO. The sands are advancing into the sea, and it is now some way inland, from the sea shore.

Not far away was the whaling ship *Eagle*. It was a wooden ship so little remains except for the wooden keel with some copper bolts in it, and the outside of the wooden keel that is coated with badly corroded metal.

Just along the beach a live drama was unfolding. There was a helicopter on the beach from Starlight Aviation. A ship had gone aground offshore. Its hold was full of frozen tuna, but it was leaking diesel. There was a tugboat offshore, standing guard and there were engineers on board, who had been taken there by a helicopter to try to mend the leak and to clear up the spillage, before the tug could move in and try to pull the boat into deeper water on the next high tide.

From there on, there was just flat sandy desert, unchanging for mile after mile. We stopped for lunch opposite another wreck; a former trawler that had run aground in 2008, which was being battered by strong waves.

We had another sixty kilometres to reach Swakopmund and what a change, compared to the other towns we had passed through! It is a microcosm of an ordered Germanic township transported to Africa. It was an even greater contrast than that experienced at the border.

There is as much German spoken here as English. There are white faces of both tourists and locals in the streets. The streets are neat, tidy and they have trees, flowers and grass in the central reservations. There were modern individual houses, surrounded by manicured gardens, with trees and palms for shade. They had garages and cars which were mostly parked in the garages, and the driveways and the streets opposite the houses were free of parked vehicles. There were street lamps. The streets were clean and free of litter and dust, despite being in a desert area. The cars were modern recent designs, clean and shiny with recently waxed surfaces sparkling in the sun.

There were industry and commercial areas arranged in neat industrial estates. There were clean delivery vehicles with logos of local firms, dropping off goods. The people were well dressed and would not look out of place on any European city street. Workers wore company uniforms or overalls, with the logo on the left breast and across the back. People wore shoes and none of the clothes were dirty, threadbare or torn, except perhaps the overlanders.

The buildings were all neatly painted and well maintained. The roads are set out in an orderly grid pattern, and all had their names on signs at every corner, something that I realised I had not seen in Africa over the previous four months of travel. Despite being largely of modern design, there was a distinct Bavarian or Germanic feel. Most of the city is single or double-storey with just a few buildings in the central business district being three stories. There were several church spires of Catholic and Lutheran churches. Except for a few street names of famous local African celebrities, you might think that you were in a Bavarian Alpine town.

The town was founded by Major Curt von François in 1892 and it was to be the harbour for the colony. It was not the ideal place, but other sites had even more disadvsntages and nearby Walvis Bay was in British hands. It was the nearest coastline to the capital, Windhoek over three hundred and fifty kilometres inland. A railway was built to connect the two which was started in 1897 and completed in 1902. There was some urgency as transport up to that point, had been by ox cart, but an outbreak of rinderpest killed off all the oxen.

Just seventy kilometres outside of the town is the Rössing Uranium Mine, which is the largest open cast uranium mine in the world, the fifth largest producer of uranium, producing ten percent of world output, making Namibia one of the top five world exporters. For TV and film buffs; the town was used to film 'The Prisoner' and 'The Village' and 'Mad Max: Fury Road'.

The town is a centre for adventure activity and adrenalin sports. There are scenic flights over the countryside and along the coast. There are acrobatic flights and sky diving for the thrill seekers. There is horse riding along a dried-up riverbed, and into the desert. Out amongst the dunes, there is sand boarding, fat tyre mountain biking and quad biking on offer.

At sea, there are kayaking options along the coast and cruises to see dolphins and seals. There are fishing expeditions and anglers can keep everything that they catch. The Benguela current is rich in minerals and wildlife, and there are big sports fish to catch just offshore.

For those less keen on adrenalin sports, there are township tours and tours to see how the different local tribes live traditionally; not to mention the large range of restaurants, cafés and bars on offer. The town attracts a lot of visitors from both the local area and from abroad, and it is a popular destination being Namibia's most visited destination.

We would be here for several days, so it was an opportunity to find a laundry to get our clothes properly washed. I went with Noodles and we found a vegetarian restaurant which had a range of dishes, and it was reasonably priced, but was not open in the evening. It was in the former Otavi railway station, which was built on what was then the outskirts of the town.

The Otavi Mining and Railway Company, shortened to OMEG, built a six hundred millimetre narrow gauge railway from the port via Otavi, across five hundred and sixty-seven kilometres of desert to Tsumeb, whose deep mine produces copper, lead and zinc ores. It is now called the Ongopolo Mine and is owned and operated by a British company.

Construction of the Otavi railway occurred between 1903 and 1906. Construction was interrupted due to the Herero and the Namaqua wars, genocide, labour shortages and military operations. A ninety-one kilometre extension was built from Otavi to Grootfontein in 1908. South African troops captured Swakopmund in January 1915, but the Germans had destroyed the track as they retreated. Therefore, the South Africans built a one thousand and sixty-seven millimetre gauge track along the same route to Karibib, about a quarter of the distance to Otavi. The mine closed in 1933, but it was reopened in 1936, as Germany was rearming. It was closed as enemy property in 1940, but it reopened in 1946, and it still produces ore. An interesting aside is that service was interrupted in 1924, due to a plaque of locusts. Their crushed bodies meant that there was no traction. The solution was to add steam blowers to blow the locusts off the track.

Now the tracks have been lifted, but the building remains and is a vegetarian restaurant and a garden centre. We then took a short walk into the centre of town to change money. We passed a Brauhaus which was a local micro-brewery, so we stopped, and we sampled several of their beers.

We then walked down to the Butcher and Brewery, another micro-brewery to meet Mat, Sarah and Jacci. They were sitting in the sun, overlooking the beach and the harbour. I had a couple of drinks and then I left, to visit the Swakopmund Museum. It had something for everyone; a video presentation on the history of Namibia, archaeology, history, geology, uniforms, photos of the town since its inception and several reproduction shops with what they sold when they were first established. There was a detailed history of the development of the town since it was founded in 1882. There were exhibits on the development of the railways and the mining industry, principally uranium, diamond, copper, lead, zinc and precious and semi-precious stones and a host of other minerals, including gold.

Gold was first discovered in Namibia in 1899, but the grade of the ores was low and there was no gold rush and commercial mining was abandoned. However, gold was discovered near Karibib in 1984 and the Navachab Gold Mine was developed. Ore grades are about one and a half percent to two percent and its annual production is about sixty-five thousand ounces. For years this was the only gold mine in Namibia but B2Gold opened the Otjikoto mine in Otjozondjupa in 2007 and has an annual production of over a hundred and eighty-nine thousand ounces.

I walked to the far side of town to visit the Hauptbahnhof, the original old station which is now a four-star hotel. The reception area and the bar are original, and it gives an idea of how plush the station was when it was first constructed. I then walked inland, and I saw the newer station. This was built when the original station was sold off and converted into a hotel. But there are no tracks here now, as the railway had been realigned and now this breeze block-built station is standing by itself, in an industrial park.

The latest passenger station is another four hundred metres further on, but it is only a platform and a couple of ramps. The train track is three metres away from the edge of the platform and there are reinforcing rods sticking out of the flat concrete. There are three trains a week between Swakopmund and Windhoek, but since the tracks have been realigned, another station needs to be built. The trains run overnight, so I was not tempted, even though I like rail travel as I can look out of the window at the scenery but I would see little on an overnight journey.

I treated myself to a game platter at the Neapolitanas. It is a taste of some of the wild meat available. It consists of small steaks of kudu, springbok, eland and kudu. They were all good, a bit like venison, but the differences aren't so great that I could pass a blind tasting.

After several days in a bed in a hostel, it seemed odd to be back on the truck. We stopped at a supermarket for supplies. It was a Sunday and the law in Namibia means that no alcohol is sold in shops after midday on Saturday and all-day Sunday. We stopped on the edge of town at the museum whose central exhibit is the Luther King steam engine, which I had learnt about at the Swakopmund Museum. It had been unloaded in Walvis Bay just down the coast. It had taken three months to drive the thirty kilometres to nearby Swakopmund where it got stuck and was abandoned a century ago. This museum housed the reconstructed engine, surrounded by paraphernalia from the period.

We then drove to the Naukluft National Park which at nearly fifty thousand square kilometres is the fourth largest in the world and comprises a large area of the Namib desert. There are several things to see here and there are numbered posts by the side of the road so that you can be certain that you are in the correct place, and your guide pamphlet will advise you of what there is to see.

There was lichen that changes colour when it gets wet from black to green. The natural covering has gone from this area, but it grows on the few boulders and posts that have been left here to show the tourists. There are lookouts over moon like mountains, a place where the South African army camped when they occupied and defeated the German colonial forces in the First World War. There was a black basalt intrusion that stretched across the top of the hills, noticeably darker in colour, and forms the tops of the hills and the ridges, as it is more resistant to erosion.

There was a campsite where there were some trees with some parasitic plants growing on them in the dried-up bed of the Swakop River. There were two types of arid resistant shrubs, small bushes, one with leaves the size and the shape of dollar coins and the other shrub with no leaves. It drops them after it has rained and flowers, to conserve moisture. Further on there were some giant Welwitschia plants, the national plant of Namibia and the oldest specimen is estimated to be fifteen hundred years old. It was named after Austrian doctor and botanist Fredrich Welwitsch, who was the first European to describe the plant that he had found in 1859 in Angola.

The last stop was to view a large hole in the ground. This was all that was left of an iron ore mine. It was dug by hand to reach the iron ore, but it was closed in the 1950s when it became uneconomical to operate.

We then drove deep into the desert in search of a campsite. We had booked with Namibian Wildlife Reserves, but you only book a campsite, which are restricted in number, but you don't book a specific location, just one in the park. We crossed a river bed and got stuck in the sand. We had to get the sand mats out to inch forward, to get back to more solid ground that could support the truck. We saw two natural stone arches, large enough to walk under and despite being smaller than the iconic arches in Arches National Park in Utah, I still found them fascinating. The camp site we were aiming for was occupied as was the next. In that case it was going to be Plan C.

We had to drive back through the soft sand of the river bed, using the sand mats and some way along another valley, to reach an unoccupied campsite. It is all national park and you are only allowed to camp at designated sites. The only facility that is provided is a long drop, some waste bins and a concrete hearth which is the only place where you can make a fire.

It was a lovely sunset with the last rays of the sun lighting up the walls of the valley before it finally went dark. Surprising for us and a unique experience is that it rained twice during the night. Thick dark clouds drifted over and obscured the stars, and the rising moon. It was never heavy rain, but it was noisy under canvas but it was only a light sprinkling. The splatters of the rain drops didn't even join up to make the nearby rock look wet. The clouds came over, dropped a few raindrops and then rushed on somewhere else, to drop their full load.

I was up early, and I climbed to the top of the nearest hill to watch the sun rise. The clouds had largely blown over but there were a few stragglers. The sky turned from grey to yellow to red before more clouds blew in, and by breakfast time the sky was overcast again.

We drove north through the desert towards the capital, Windhoek. As we drove the road rose into the hills and we crossed several passes, one with a marvellous lookout at one thousand five hundred and twenty-five metres. The vegetation also changed, as the mountains had more rainfall and it had rained within the last few weeks. There were the same shrubs, but they looked more vigourous. There was also a thin covering of grass and some yellow and mauve flowers.

I had seen this before when after a heavy downpour, the desert comes to life and the normally bare sand is covered with flowers and grasses which make the most of the sudden downpour. The desert turns green in just two weeks, and there is an abundance of flowers. The sudden greenery attracts zebra and eland and other large game, which in turn attracts hyenas and lions. Insects come out to pollinate and to eat one another, bees collect pollen and the mass of insects attracts birds. Then, in just another two weeks it turns brown, and the hot sun desiccates the flowers and the grasses, and it returns to sandy seemingly lifeless desert.

The road suddenly reverted to tarmac, and it descends out of the hills and down to Windhoek at an elevation of one thousand six hundred and fifty-five metres. The city was founded in 1840 by Jonker Afrikaner, captain of the *Orlam* with his three brothers and with three hundred settlers at the site of a hot spring. He built a stone church for the community, but tribal warfare caused the settlement to be abandoned. The city was founded a second time by Major Curt von François in 1890 when he laid the first stone for the Alte Feste or Old Fortress, he was the same person who founded Swakopmund.

It was another public holiday, so the shops were shut so we couldn't shop, and several restaurants were either closed or full, so we made do with a toasty at the bar of the hostel.

Breakfast was advertised as seven a.m. but we were still waiting at seven thirty a.m. for coffee, hot water and bread. The staff seemed to be in no hurry but then again, TIA stands for 'This is Africa' meaning that this is not exceptional, but it was a little different from the Germanic feel of Swakopmund.

I walked into the city centre to see a few of the sights and my first stop was the railway station. There was some contemporary rolling stock but also some older engines and wagons on display. There were some timetables, but the trains are irregular, and I couldn't work out a route to go somewhere and to be back before we would be moving on again.

I visited the National Art Gallery to view its collection of largely contemporary and modern art. The few items aroused a little interest but much of it didn't appeal. Next door is the National Theatre and next to that is the Owela Museum which was previously known as the Landes museum. It had a lot of Namibian wildlife exhibits, anthropology and it showed how the locals lived in peace and harmony before colonisation by Germany in 1884. It has so much to do with the local population, the culture and the wildlife and it is a more ethnographic museum than anything to do with Owela which I had had explained to me a week before.

Indeed, many of the exhibits, clothes, tools, blacksmith skills, leather making, beads and the like were very similar to what I had already seen at the Damara Cultural Museum. It was interesting, but too many of the light bulbs were missing, so some of the exhibits could only be seen and read in the glow from adjacent exhibits, and other exhibits were shrouded in darkness.

I walked through Zoo Park which is a favourite place to amble through in the shade on a hot day, past the parliament building and opposite it, the Christuskirche, the city cathedral. Dominating the top of the hill was the Museum of Independence. It is a modern triangular building standing on three stilts, one in each corner. The entrance is flanked by two statues, one of Sam Nujoma, the first president of Namibia, and a memorial, the Genocide Statue.

There are three floors of exhibits depicting different eras such as pre-colonial, the colonial exploitation, the UN mandate, followed by the struggle for independence and finally total independence. The fourth floor is a reasonably priced restaurant with panoramic views of the city, and the fifth floor is not open to the public.

I walked back through the city and I looked around some of the malls and the old brewery. I found a bar selling a range of local craft beers and I sampled several. I had a meal in an overpriced restaurant and I wished that I had returned to the restaurant at the Museum of Independence with its views over the city.

Meanwhile Kim had gone to the South African embassy to reapply for a visa in person. Her original application had been rejected, so she was doing the 'tearful trapped tourist begging weepy eyed plead' in person thing. Her application had been accepted and her work permit stamped, but that didn't mean that she had been granted a visa, only that they had taken her money and she would not discover the result for another week.

We left Windhoek at midday and drove south west through yet more desert, and a couple of bush camps with the aim of arriving at Lüderitz. We turned off the main highway and headed across some high plateau desert through Klein Aud, Rietoog towards Maltahöhe. This town was founded by Henning von Burgsdorff, a former officer in the Schutztruppe, who named it after his wife Malta.

We found a flat spot next to the road for a bush camp. It wasn't ideal but we were in the middle of nowhere. There was little traffic on the road, and after we stopped, only one vehicle came past between late afternoon and packing away the camp and getting back on the road in the morning.

Whilst packing away the kitchen the night before, a lone local walked past. We hadn't seen any buildings but there were occasional signs pointing to a farm hidden in the hills down a track that led away from the main track. He explained that he had been to a party and that he was walking home. I asked if he worked on this farm, but he said no, the next one. Since each farm can be thousands of hectares; in order to make a living from the sparse desert grazing, he still had a long way to go.

There was still no traffic on the road, and it was more of the same desert. Mid-morning, we turned off the main road and stopped in Maltahöhe. It was no more than a village, but it had a bank and a supermarket, so we stocked up and were soon back on the road.

We stopped at Duwisib Castle. It is set back from the road and it is a modern reproduction of a medieval castle with a tower and battlements. It is part museum and part hotel. Hans Heinrich von Wolf and his wife Jayta commissioned the building of the castle. Heinrich was born to Major General Ernst Hugo von Wolf and Caroline Louise on the 11th of January 1873. Their portraits hang in the dining room.

Hans Heinrich served in the Royal Saxon Artillery for the King of Saxony at Königbrück. Towards the end of 1904 he was voluntarily transferred to the Schutztruppe in what was then German South West Africa. He served as a captain in command of a regiment. It was during this time that he developed an interest in the Maltahöhe area. In 1906 he resigned his commission and returned to Germany.

His wife was born Jayta Humphrey in Summit, New Jersey in 1881. After her father's death, her mother married the American consul to Germany who was stationed at Dresden. Jayta inherited a fortune from her grandfather and by the time that she married Hans Heinrich she was a millionaire.

They married on the 8th of April 1907 and they chose Namibia as their new home. They arrived in Windhoek in mid-1907 and bought the Duwisib farm from the Treasury. Work started on the castle the following year, and more land was bought to expand the estate to fifty-five thousand hectares. The castle was completed in 1909.

The couple lived in the castle from 1909 to 1914. Local people had already started calling them Baron and Baroness, honorific titles befitting their lifestyle. Hans Heinrich bred horses from imported Australian and British stock. Two of his famous stallions were Cracker Jack and Benito. Local people and the government used his bloodlines to improve their horses. He imported two Hereford bulls from England to improve his cattle herd. He also had a flock of wool sheep imported from the Cape Colony.

They employed seven Europeans who assisted them in the running of their farm enterprises and their household. The accountant, lady in waiting, seamstress, chef, butler and others lived in the series of interlinked rooms in the western flank of the castle.

During 1914 the couple left Lüderitz for England, to buy another stallion for their stud farm, leaving their farm in the hands of a friend. While at sea they learnt of the outbreak of war in Europe in August 1914. The German liner that they were travelling on had to find sanctuary and sailed to Rio de Janeiro where they were interned.

After some months they were released and found passage on a neutral ship back to Europe. Hans Heinrich was determined that he should join the German forces protecting his motherland. The couple escaped being discovered when their Dutch registered ship was detained by the British Navy in Southampton, and Hans Heinrich hid in a trunk to avoid detection when the ship was searched. Eventually they reached Rotterdam and they crossed the border into Germany. Hans Heinrich re-joined the army but on the 4th of September 1916, he was killed during the Battle of the Somme near Le Forêt.

Jayta stayed in Munich and she remarried sometime between the two world wars. During the Second World War, she moved to Switzerland, and after the war, she returned to Summit, New York. She died there in 1946 at the age of sixty-four.

She had never returned to Duwisib to lay claim to her property, her personal possessions or to the estate. In 1920, the farm had been sold to a Swedish family named Murman. Mr Murman passed away suddenly in the castle. His son was a South African Air Force pilot who was shot down during the Second World War. So there seems to be a bit of bad luck associated with the castle.

The farm, castle and contents were then sold to the Thorer Group. They used the castle as a residence for their farm manager until 1979 when the government bought the castle to be kept as part of their National Heritage.

The castle was designed by Wilheim Sander. It complies with the Wilhelminian neo romantic style and contains some Gothic and Renaissance elements. The red sandstone for the castle was obtained from a hill behind the castle. Local Herero people were employed for the quarrying and to work on the site. Italian stonemasons finished off the stone and built the castle. Carpenters from Germany, Sweden and Belgium were responsible for the woodwork. The castle has twenty-two rooms and covers nine hundred square metres.

All the other building material was imported from Europe. This was transported by ox wagon from Lüderitz, which was the harbour that was nearest to the castle by ox wagon driven by neighbouring Afrikaans speaking farmers. Considering that the castle was finished in under two years, this was a remarkable feat.

The entrance to the castle is through the tower. The vestibule leads into the Knight's Hall. Above the vestibule is the gallery. On the left are the Biedermeier and the dining rooms. The Von Wolffs private rooms are to the right.

They collected antique furniture and imported Jugendstil furniture and there is still a complete set in the castle. Besides furniture, the castle was decorated with excellent paintings, copperplate engravings, photographs and ornamental weapons. Hans Heinrich's passion for horses is well reflected in the numerous paintings of the horses still hanging on the walls.

We drove on to a campsite in the middle of nowhere, not far from a crossroads. It had hot water, showers, clean toilets, barbecue pits, running water in the sinks next to each pitch and vast stretches of desert in all directions to distant mountains. But there was a drawback as at this time of year, the wind picks up in the afternoon and blows until dusk. And in the early morning, it picks up from the opposite direction until perhaps an hour after sunrise. So, wherever you pitch your tent, behind whatever shrub or wall you may find, you will still feel the wind.

CHAPTER 22
LÜDERITZ AND THE KOLMANSKOP GHOST TOWN

There was a lovely sunrise, as we packed up and drove just a hundred and seventy-two kilometres to the first stop at Aus, to get some supplies and personally to get a take away coffee. It is a lovely picture postcard little hamlet, set in a narrow valley where the train tracks start to climb into hills after crossing the desert. However, it was a prisoner of war detention centre from 1915 until the end of the war, when the prisoners were deported to Germany. There is a beautiful little church, a Bahnhof Hotel, a general store and a couple of houses.

Then there was a long flat drive across the desert. There was a railway running alongside the road, sometimes nearby, sometimes taking an alternative route around a hill. There were no trains while we were on the road, but this was not surprising as there are no commercial trains. The track fell into disrepair decades ago, but it is being upgraded and services are due to be re-introduced. The original track took just ten months to lay between Lüderitz and Aus which is on the mainline using Herero forced labour, and prisoners of war from the rebellion. Work has been going on to replace and to upgrade the track for the past ten years, but it is due to open soon but only after some of the sand dunes that have since covered the track have been removed, and the final signalling apparatus installed.

There are signs reminding drivers that they are not allowed to leave the road as it is a diamond concession. We stopped near Lüderitz to visit the Kolmanskop Diamond Mining Ghost Town. We had obtained our permit to visit as the ghost town is technically in the diamond concession area where entry is forbidden without a permit. There are numerous buildings, all now being lost to the drifting dunes. They are in various stages of disrepair, but some have been preserved.

The whole town was originally set up to mine diamonds. The first geologists were looking for copper but missed the diamonds as they had never previously been found in sand. A worker handed an unusual rock to a geologist who correctly identified the unusual specimen as a diamond; and there were more diamonds literally lying on the ground.

There followed a diamond rush, as it was so easy to just pick them up. The diamonds had been washed here to form beach terraces which have since been covered by drifting sand dunes. With better geological techniques employed, new deposits were discovered, and mining moved further south, and the mining town was abandoned.

There are stories of people trying to smuggle diamonds out. No expense was spared for the diamond mining town and they had the first x-ray machine in the southern hemisphere in their large and well-equipped hospital, partly to see broken bones but it was also used to check the workers leaving the concession, to check for diamonds.

Laden Strasse was the main street and it is where the shopkeeper's house was located. Anything and everything was available. If it wasn't in stock then the storekeeper would telephone an order back to Germany, and it would arrive on the next ship. There was a Kegelbahn, a bowling alley in one of the buildings for entertainment. They had their own theatre with top quality acts enticed to perform on the stage for stupendous amounts of money but the diamond mine was so profitable that it could afford the best acts. Some of the first movies shown anywhere in the world were shown here. The town had three hundred Germans and the school educated forty-four children. There were also eight hundred local contract workers.

The sand dunes are reclaiming the town. They are blowing in and covering the buildings. The sand heaps up on one side and blows through the windows and fills the rooms. Some of the houses are in danger of collapsing under the weight of the sand. There are plenty of excellent photo opportunities of sand heaped up in corners. Many of the original features are still in situ, as the place was abandoned and there was no one nearby to plunder the buildings. There was an ice plant and electricity was generated by burning coal in nearby Lüderitz and transmitting power to the site. Despite only having a few hundred expats, they had a tram system to take the married women from the married quarters to the shops and back.

The restored railway line passes near the Kolmanskop Diamond Mine and terminates in Lüderitz on the coast. Lüderitz was founded in 1883 when Heinrich Vogelsang purchased the bay then called Angra Pequena, on behalf of Adolf Lüderitz, a prominent citizen and trader from Bremen in Germany. When Adolf Lüderitz did not return from a trip to the Orange River, the town was renamed Lüderitzbucht in his honour.

There is a restored railway station ready to receive trains when the line is opened; and an original carriage standing in the sidings in the town centre. There is a church on a hill, overlooking the town and most of the architecture in the town is art deco. Many of the houses have their dates of construction displayed near the apex of the roof or above the door.

There was a museum in the town. There were exhibits of local animals, about the Bushmen, diamond mining, local history and loads of photos. There was also information on Shark Island, which was a peninsula on which Herero prisoners of war were interred in conditions like a concentration camp. It is a desolate, windswept stony peninsula with no shade and no water. There are dangerous currents off shore so escape by sea was impossible and it was easy for a few German soldiers to guard the fence between Shark Island and the mainland.

It was at Shark Island where German anthropologists Doctor Fischer and Doctor Bofinger conducted eugenic fieldwork, personally decapitating seventeen dead prisoners and examining the skulls, and weighing the brains as part of their experimentations, to prove that the Herero and the Namaqua were not human, but a form of sub-species and they had the support of Heinrich Göring, then the Governor General of German South West Africa and father of Herman Göring, the Second World War Nazi commander of the Luftwaffe. The doctors later went to work in Berlin and they would have crossed paths with Doctor Josef Mengele who undertook eugenics and medical research in Auschwitz.

Today the area is a campsite with several memorials to shipwreck victims, explorers, local heroes and to the first German settlers who were killed by the Herero when they rebelled against their colonial overlords.

We were going to have a barbecue in the evening at our hostel. On the way back from Shark Island I passed the local supermarket which was shut, despite it being a Saturday; but Saturday is a half day shopping day in Namibia, and no alcohol can be bought at the weekend after Saturday midday.

I also passed the local fish shop. They had had a recent delivery from some fishermen and there was kingklip on offer. This is a wonderful solid white flesh fish that I had tried in a restaurant in Swakopmund. I bought four times the amount for a quarter of the price that I had paid for in the restaurant. I was elated as I had got a good deal and I shared the succulent fish at the barbecue. The only downer on the evening was that there were some Germans also staying at the hostel and they helped themselves to our cold beers, and we only realised the theft when we went to pack up the next morning and we found that our beer supplies for the next couple of days had been drunk.

We hit the supermarket at eight a.m. for supplies and Jacci and I blew the budget yet again but at least it was only a few dollars over. It's our responsibility to shop so we had to cover the extra. But we felt it more important to have ice to keep the meat fresh and paprika for the goulash.

We drove out of town and we stopped to see some flamingos' feeding in the shallows. There were also gulls, ducks and other water fowl. We stopped at Diaz Cross. This is across set up by Portuguese explorers as they made their way around the coast of Africa, in search of a sea route to India and further unexplored or unclaimed lands. The original cross was made of wood but was replaced with a stone cross erected here by Bartolomeu Diaz on the 27th of July 1488 as a navigation aid, as there were few other distinguishing points of reference for sailors and the coast of Africa and the stars in the southern hemisphere were still largely unknown, so it was the pilot's secret book and these crosses that helped him to guide ships into the unknown.

There were seals on an offshore island where they felt safe from humans and could relax or sleep. The sea was rough, and it would be very difficult to get to the island by boat even if it wasn't far. There was a footbridge to another island that was a lookout over the seal island, but it had been washed away by storms in 2012. A new one had been designed and there was a charity to collect donations to pay for the replacement. It crosses an area that floods at high tide, but the island gives a good view of the seal island and with binoculars you can see many of the sea birds that nest on the island.

On another island there was a colony of Fairy Penguins. They were difficult to see with the naked eye, but with binoculars, we could just about see them, but my camera wasn't powerful enough to take any meaningful photos.

We returned to Lüderitz and we took the road through the diamond concession. We pulled off the road at a designated picnic spot which was also a watering hole for local wildlife and for the horses that had escaped from von Wolfs Duwisib Castle Estate. Now they roam the desert and do quite well, but after several years of drought, they are fed by the Namib Wild Horse Society, who put out bales of hay at three points and ensure that there is water available to keep them alive.

The older horses are not in good condition as they are used to wandering and they do not stay long enough at the feeding sites. The younger horses have learnt to wait for passing tourists and picnickers and they don't get enough roughage in their diet. There are signs to say not to feed the horses, but obviously enough tourists are irresponsible enough to ignore the notices and they feed the horses while picnicking, with potentially devastating results.

We stopped in Aus at the garage shop for a takeaway coffee. Then we drove into the desert. There were rain clouds chasing us through some very picturesque scenery from Aus alongside the railway to Goaged, and towards Keetmanshoop, but the adventure slowed again as the monotonous desert took over again.

We then took a side turning and we made a bush camp. We had been running away from darkening rain clouds all afternoon, but now they thickened on both sides of us. There was lightning on both sides, but a small patch of blue lay just above us.

Our plan was to camp here, to be near the Fish River Canyon to visit it in the morning and to stay at the eco-lodge there. This wasn't on our original plan, but we had some enforced extra days, due to the South African embassy's mistake on Gareth's visa which was dated a few days later than had been scheduled. Imbe and Chris were over the moon, as they would be leaving the truck in Cape Town and they were looking at how to visit the canyon by themselves; but it was inaccessible by public transport so they would have to hire a car and take several days to drive north and back again, which was both expensive and impacted on their other travel plans. So, they were overjoyed with how events had panned out.

Imbe was cooking by herself. There had been another rearrangement of the cook groups and she was partnerless but she didn't mind, as she knew that people would help. Everything was going well until there was a sudden gust of wind. It blew my tent over and along the ground. It ripped out the tent pegs, broke one of the rubber rings that hold the outer canvas onto the pegs and tore some of the stitching apart at the apex of the flysheet.

The wind also hit the side of the truck and lifted the awning off its central steel pole which fell and hit Imbe on the head. She collapsed straight away, groaning but conscious. There was a lot of blood as head injuries always seem to bleed so much worse than other wounds. It was a deep gash and worse than just a lump of ice to cope with it. She needed a hospital. We packed everything away and drove the hundred and forty kilometres to the nearest medical centre, which was in Keetmanshoop. She was seen straight away. They had to cut her hair which despite the wound, she was not happy about, but the doctor needed to see the wound clearly.

She had to have five stitches and she was then discharged. It was late at night and we had no hope of finding another campsite and we wanted to stay close to the medical facility in case of a relapse with Imbe or her going into shock. We asked and we were given permission to camp in the car park opposite, if we were packed away early. We moved on from the car park shortly after dawn for the short journey to the town campsite.

At the town campsite there was plenty of hot water and after Chris had got some hot water in a bowl and washed Imbe's hair carefully around the wound, she felt better. Although she was still concerned that her bald patch would be visible for months, as her hair only grew slowly.

I walked into town past the town museum, which was housed in a church. This church had been built in 1890 to replace an earlier church that had been washed away in a flood. The town got its name from Johan Keetman. He was a prosperous trader in Barman who made a generous donation to a missionary called Doctor Hugo Hahn, in 1860 to build the church as a mission, because it was his hope that the missionary would convert the local Namaqua people to Christianity. The museum had a modest entry fee and it has exhibits about the local fauna, flora, local culture and some exhibits from colonial times. It is also ecclesiastically unusual, as the pulpit is located behind the altar in the centre of the church.

Around the corner was a newer church. It is distinctive as it is in an art deco style with a tall modern square tower seen from the outside, but hexagonal inside, with pews on three sides, facing the altar and a circular upper gallery. It was a fascinating place but without any plaque or information, I was lost as to its history. I had earlier been challenged to give a date of construction, as I had often viewed other buildings and told interested people the probable date and type of construction. For this church,

I plumped for 1924 as the date of construction, but I wasn't far wrong as the earliest gravestone that I could find in the cemetery was dated 1928.

We cooked lunch for Imbe as, although she was feeling better, it was her turn to produce a meal, and we didn't expect her to prepare lunch by herself if she was injured, so we insisted that she sit in the shade and we all mucked in to prepare lunch.

Then Gareth drove Kim, Gavin, Elle and me out to a site that promised to show us some quiver trees, and to the 'Giants Play Ground'. We had to drive up a gravel track for twenty-three kilometres to see one of the local popular tourist destinations at the Mesosaurus Camp.

It was run by Giel, an Afrikaner who had bought the farm in 1972 and has run it ever since. His son now runs the farm, but Giel still takes tourists around the local sites as a tour guide. The farm had sheep and goats, but it has a stocking rate of one animal per five hectares as the forage is so poor but it also explains why the farms are so large. At home in the United Kingdom we might find ten animals per hectare. The farm was surrounded by electric fences to keep hyenas and jackals away from the flocks, but there were still plenty of hyrax to eat the vegetation and to compete with the sheep and goats.

Giel was a character and told several anecdotes. The usual trip was for him to drive his vehicle and for the tourists to follow in their own vehicles. However only Kim, Jacci and I wanted to do the tour, so we squeezed into his 4x4. Gareth wanted to do some work on the truck and Gavin and Elle had only come along for the ride and to chill out somewhere different from the camp and the town.

So, we were squeezed into Giel's pickup and he drove us across his farm to the first stop, which was next to the grave of a Schutztruppe who had been killed here in an ambush, by some rebellious Herero who they were tracking. There was another grave on the other side of the hill of another Schutztruppe who was killed during the same ambush. The incident was reported in detail in the Swakopmund Press newspaper at the time.

There are numerous fossils in the area that date from two hundred and eighty million years ago. They are between thirty-five centimetres and one metre in length and lived in a shallow salty sea. There are loads of specimens that even a school child could find.

Above us there were the huge nests of communal weaver birds which can house up to a hundred pairs, with each pair having their own entrance. Plus, most communal nests also host a pygmy falcon, who also lives in the nest but is tolerated as he protects the nest from snakes and lizards.

The area is covered with the tips of an enormous igneous intrusion with pinpricks of magma penetrating the overlying rock. These had weathered into blocks, balanced on top of one another. This gives the impression of a child who has piled several blocks on top of one another, and hence the name for the area, 'the Giants Play Ground'.

Giel demonstrated how some of the rocks 'sing' when hit. There was a set of rocks which had just the right resonances to produce a range of notes to play several recognisable tunes including 'Happy Birthday' and a popular African tune. Giel made it seem so easy. I banged at other balanced rocks, but try as hard as I could I could only find a few that sung, and even fewer rocks that made a melodious sound. The group of balanced rocks that Giel had shown us are unique in being able to play a recognisable tune.

We were surrounded by quiver trees. They have a single stem and they only split into two branches after twenty to twenty-five years. And then each branch splits into two so the trees have dense and regularly curved dome-like canopies. But one was unusual, as it sprouted several branches from the ground. On closer inspection, we saw that it had been blown over but had survived and had grown new roots, so its branches grew out of the ground and gave it a unique character.

The quiver tree is named after its most useful purpose, which is to make a quiver to hold arrows. The central core is made of a soft wood with a frail membrane inside. The tree can suck up water after a rain storm and it can store it in its trunk. But around the core of the tree is a hard section, followed by another section that is soft and flexible, before reaching the outer bark. It is the inner hard section that is sought after, and with the inner soft membrane removed and separated from the rest of the shaft, it makes a solid wood tube which when one end is closed with leather, makes an excellent quiver for arrows.

We moved on to Felix Unite River Adventures, crossing a dry empty desert until we were near the river. In Namibia only the Orange and the Fish Rivers flow all year round and provide plenty of water to irrigate fields and therefore provide locals with jobs and a product to trade.

We turned through the gates of Felix Unite River Adventures and after lunch, we did a truck clean which lasted all afternoon. This truck clean included taking all the seats out, so it was five hours of cleaning, wiping and sweeping, and then when everything had dried, it all had to be put back. It also required that all the tents be put up and washed inside and out.

After such long hard labour in high temperatures, it was time to relax and most people headed to the bar for the evening, for drinks to celebrate the truck clean and then they drifted off to bed.

Sometime, during the next day, we crossed the Tropic of Capricorn but there was no sign at the side of the road. Kim left that evening for the night bus to Windhoek to go to the South African embassy to discover whether she had been given a visa. On the assumption that she had got a visa, she would take the night bus back to the camp site.

It was a free day at the Felix Unite River Adventures camp site. There were options to kayak or to canoe down the river. We would be taken upriver in a bus, with the kayaks on the back of the trailer and then paddle down the river for the day and get out at the riverside campsite.

At the campsite there were some excellent facilities, a restaurant with a varied menu, flat grass covered camping pitches, plus the opportunity to upgrade to dormitories, cabins or even upmarket luxury cabins, many overlooking the river, as it flowed westwards to the sea. There was also an opportunity for a four-day camping and canoe trip downriver but however much I wanted to do this, there was not enough time on this trip.

I had a lazy day of doing nothing. I walked around the resort and I checked out the restaurant, the shop and the swimming pool although the pool was very green, and you couldn't see the bottom. I didn't want to get in, just in case I caught something.

I walked around the cabins and if I were to come back another time, I would insist on having Cabin Number Four with its own patio overlooking the river. It was also slightly bigger than the others and it was probably the most expensive but that would be my choice when I returned. Later, after meeting up with the other in the group, I found myself back at the bar, and after a long hot afternoon, and with my judgement impaired by being at the bar for a few hours, I went for a swim to cool off in the green slime. Luckily, I survived without any detrimental effects.

CHAPTER 23
SOUTH AFRICA

We crossed the Orange River which forms the border between Namibia and South Africa. Then a long drive across more desert but on excellent roads to Highlanders. Initially, the scenery was just desert, but as we came down from the highlands and there was more water, there were flat fields of irrigated crops in the bottom of the valley and further down the valley and as there was more water, there were irrigated fields up the sides of the valley. Many of the fields are planted with vines and it is a major wine producing area.

By the time we got to Trawal the valley bottoms were continuous fields. Highlanders is a small vineyard that has camping facilities and holds wine tastings, which we all signed up for. There were six wines, a white, three reds, a sweet desert wine and a digestif, a strong locally distilled spirit. It was a busy evening as other tour companies had guests at the campsite.

We had a leisurely breakfast and were the last group to leave Highlanders. We drove through the Cederburg Wilderness via Clanwilliam, Ceres, Worcester and Bredasdorp to Cape Agulhas, Portuguese for Cape Needles and a reference to a compass as the magnetic needle always points north to aid navigation. This is the most southerly point of the continent of Africa and it is also known for its fishing. Cape Agulhas is the dividing line between the warm Indian Ocean, and the cooler Atlantic Ocean with the Benguela current that flows north from Antarctica and brings mineral rich but cold water north and is known for its rich fish stocks, its Wright and humpback whales and it is also popular with fishermen.

It was late in the day and there was some low cloud, so we camped near Cape Agulhas and we hoped for better weather the next day. There was a restaurant adjacent to the camp site and they had a selection of fish on the menu. It seemed only fitting for us to skip cooking for ourselves and to celebrate especially as this was to be our last night camping as well as the end of the adventure.

Many of us were awake early not so much due to the excitement of seeing the most southerly point of the continent after travelling south for five months, but because there were two groups of fishermen at the campground. They were up early to be out on the water for sunrise and they were packing up their gear into their pickups and making quite a bit of noise, plus they were talking loudly making no effort to be quiet. There was a heavy dew which made the tents wet. They were going to be packed away as it was the end of the trip, so we had to dry them out before taking them down.

We stopped at the lighthouse which houses a museum about the history of the lighthouse; standing on the clifftop overlooking the shore. It is the second oldest lighthouse in South Africa, built in 1849 and it is thirty-one metres high, which was the highest at the time, but it is now only the thirty-first highest in the world. It is an unusual shape as it was modelled on the Pharos of Alexandria, one of the Seven Ancient Wonders of the World.

Down on the shore are signs directing visitors to a monument. This is a giant relief map of Africa and we could easily pick our route through nineteen countries, past Mount Cameroon, over major rivers such as the Congo, and to where we now stood at Cape Agulhas. Opposite is a small brass plate announcing the spot as the most southerly spot, and a line with the Indian Ocean to our left and the Atlantic Ocean to our right and in front of us a vast stretch of ocean with no land until you reach the icy wasteland of Antarctica. This was the end of the thousands of kilometres that I had covered, from the Mediterranean coast in the north to the very southern tip of the continent of Africa.

OTHER BOOKS
BY THE SAME AUTHOR

The Klondikers

The Klondikers was the name given to the people who took part in the gold rush when they heard about the gold that was to be found around what was to become Dawson City. It was just sitting there waiting to be picked up by anyone who could make the challenging journey to get there.

This is the recreation of the journey that one farmer from the wheat growing areas of the prairies around Calgary may have experienced to get to the gold.

It is the story of crossing the Rockies to the western seaboard, travelling up the coast and making landfall. Then the intrepid potential gold panner had to cross the Rockies on foot and brave blizzards and freezing cold.

When the weather and the ice had melted, he then had to paddle his way down eight hundred kilometres of river to the goldfields. Once he arrived that was the least of his problems.

K2, The Savage Mountain

This is the story of travels in northern Pakistan using Gilgit as a centre. The journey heads westward to the fascinating Kalash Valleys and a surviving unique culture struggling to live and maintain their identity in the harsh and rugged mountains bordering Afghanistan.

In the province of Baltistan and its capital Karimabad with its iconic forts of Baltit and Altit set high in the mountains the route follows the infamous Karakoram Highway through the Karakoram Mountains that links the country to China via the Khunjerab Pass, the highest road border crossing in the world.

Looking eastwards there is the Deosai plateau which has an average elevation of four thousand metres and the disputed areas of Jammu and Kashmir. Finally, there is the ascent to base camp of K2, the world's second highest but most deadly mountain.

Overlanding the Silk Road

This is the long journey that follows the Silk Road overland between Europe and China. The journey starts in London with a dash across Europe. There is a pause in Istanbul to view its many treasures and then the story winds through the history and countryside of Turkey. Then over the border into Iran to experience its rich history and architecture.

There are the bizarre experiences of the beautiful, modern but empty city of Ashgabat, the capital of Turkmenistan. Just north of the city are the Dervasa Gas Craters that are in the middle of the desert with its secret spectacular display best seen at night.

A trip to the disappearing Aral Sea is followed by an immense amount of empire building, architecture and history across a land fought over by Alexander the Great, Tamarind and Genghis Khan to name just a few of the conquerors who have roamed across this landscape.

There is an enchanting wander through the mountains of Kyrgyzstan. This country of beautiful mountains and lakes is known as Asia's little Switzerland.

The scene slowly changes as the Muslim influence gives way to Han Chinese dominance, the Great Wall of China and the end of the Silk Road at the ancient capital of Xian and its famous terracotta army.

Yellow School Bus

This is a trip from Anchorage in Alaska to Panama City in an iconic yellow school bus. There is the wild frontier landscape in Alaska and a glimpse of the Klondikers story of panning for gold in the Yukon and always with the potential danger from bears, moose and elk.

Traveling through the United States roughly following the Pan American Highway, there are stops at some of the most famous national parks such as Yellowstone and the Grand Canyon to name just two of many. There are side trips to Antelope Island and Salt Lake City and a stop off at Las Vegas for the glitz.

A nostalgic ride down Highway 66 relives some of the past and there is a visit to the meteorite crater outside Flagstaff. Over the border into Mexico there is some relaxation on the beach and a taste of Tequila.

The journey twists through Aztec and Mayan culture, over crocodile infested rivers and an oasis of English culture in Belize in an otherwise Latin American environment. There is relaxation on Caribbean islands, hunting for sloths, tasting the high life in spas and some romance as the journey weaves its way through the mountains, history and wildlife of Central America.

Crossing Russia on the Trans-Siberian

Russia is a vast country that covers more than a third of Europe and stretches for nearly nine thousand kilometres across northern Asia. The journey takes the reader on a tour through Russian culture, history and geography starting in the Imperial city of Saint Petersburg with its spectacular palaces and museums.

A voyage by ship leaves Saint Petersburg to follow rivers and canals crossing several lakes through the northern pine forests past wooden cathedrals and monasteries to join the Volga to reach Moscow. There is the Kremlin and Red Square plus many other sights including one of the largest and ugliest sculptures in the world.

After Moscow is one of the longest railway journeys in the world on the Trans-Siberian railway to pass through birch forests, over grassy steppes and through the Ural Mountains.

There are stops en route at Yekaterinburg where the Imperial family were murdered by the Bolsheviks, horse riding in the Altai Mountains to reach Mount Belukha, Siberia's highest mountain and at Irkutsk near Lake Baikal with its unique biodiversity and the world's largest volume of fresh water before finally reaching Vladivostok in Russia's far east and its port on the Pacific.

Across the Caspian

This is a tale through the Caucasus from Europe's lowest point on the shores of the Caspian Sea to its highest point on the summit of Mount Elbrus. The route follows a strand of the Silk Road from Ashgabat, the capital of Turkmenistan through the desert to reach a ferry across the Caspian to Baku.

From there the journey winds through some of the history of The Caucasus with its ancient kingdoms and the landscape of Azerbaijan and across the border into Georgia. This country is famous for its distinctive and good quality wines plus many churches and monasteries, an enclave of Christianity surrounded by populations that are predominantly Muslim.

Mount Elbrus is in Russia to the north, but the border was shut so it meant a diversion through Cappadocia in Turkey before approaching Mount Elbrus from the Russian side of the border for the attempt on the summit, which at an elevation of five thousand eight hundred and sixty-two metres is Europe's highest mountain.

Condors over Chile

The condor is associated with the Andes and this story recalls travelling down the length of the Andes and the search to see condors. From the far north of the continent on the arid Guajira peninsula, the route passes through hotspots such as Medellin and Bogota and a climb up Mount Puracé, an active volcano.

There is a break in Quito to stand on the equator. There is a fascinating visit to the Galapagos and a voyage through the islands that make up the archipelago. There is a huge array of wildlife that is not afraid of humans so you can get close to its tortoises and its other unique wildlife.

Then there is the experience of seeing some of Peru's ancient civilisations and the country of origin of more than three and a half thousand varieties of potato before continuing down the Andes to the windswept wastelands of Patagonia to Ushuaia at the end of the world in the search for the condor.

A MESSAGE
FROM THE AUTHOR

Whether you have enjoyed the book immensely or found it a useful aid to insomnia, please provide me with a little help and feedback. Amazon Books algorithms work to advertise books that they think would be of interest to other readers based on their search criteria. But they only work if they have enough data which means at least fifty reviews on the Amazon Books website.

Therefore, in order to help a struggling author, please may I ask you to write a review of this book on Amazon Books. It can be of any length, but I am not looking for a five-hundred-word review, just rate it honestly as you think fit and write what you felt about the book. You can use your own name or remain anonymous by using a pseudonym.

Thanking in you in anticipation,

Norman Handy

The author

Norman Handy was born in 1957 in Beckenham, Kent in the south east of England. He went to school in Beckenham and later went to boarding school in Cranbrook, Kent. He studied Business Economics and Accountancy, plus Law for Accountants at Southampton University.
During his studies, he also travelled and after finishing university travelled and worked abroad. He returned to the United Kingdom and after some time working in a riding school, followed a career for thirty years in the financial services sector in London, including periods working overseas.
He has two children and is a keen horse rider, walker and skier and of course, writer! He spends his time between his home in West Sussex and travelling.

novum PUBLISHER FOR NEW AUTHORS

The publisher

*He who stops
getting better
stops being good.*

This is the motto of novum publishing, and our focus is on finding new manuscripts, publishing them and offering long-term support to the authors.
Our publishing house was founded in 1997, and since then it has become THE expert for new authors and has won numerous awards.

Our editorial team will peruse each manuscript within a few weeks free of charge and without obligation.

You will find more information about
novum publishing and our books on the internet:

w w w . n o v u m - p u b l i s h i n g . c o . u k

Rate this book on our website!

www.novum-publishing.co.uk

novum PUBLISHER FOR NEW AUTHORS

Norman Handy
Overlanding the Silk Road

ISBN 978-3-99048-708-2
354 Pages

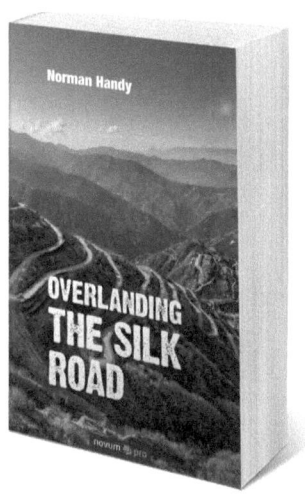

Overlanding the Silk Road is a real page turner, taking you on journeys you never thought you'd go on! From London to places like Kyrgyzstan, known as Asia's little Switzerland. Sit back and enjoy the beautiful scenery and experiences this book will take you on.

Norman Handy
The Klondikers

ISBN 978-3-99048-714-3
246 Pages

Have you ever wondered how gold is really found? Well you're about to find out as Norman Handy recreates the journey that one farmer from the wheat growing areas of the prairies around Calgary, may have experienced in his quest to find gold!

Norman Handy

K2, The Savage Mountain

Travels in Northern Pakistan

ISBN 978-3-99048-716-7
262 Pages

Strap yourself in for this one as you're in for quite a ride! This is the story of one man's travels in northern Pakistan. The final challenge comes for the ascent to the base camp of K2, the world's most deadly of mountains. A definite must read!

Norman Handy
Yellow School Bus
Adventures on a Yellow School Bus from Anchorage in Alaska to Panama

ISBN 978-3-99064-051-7
242 Pages

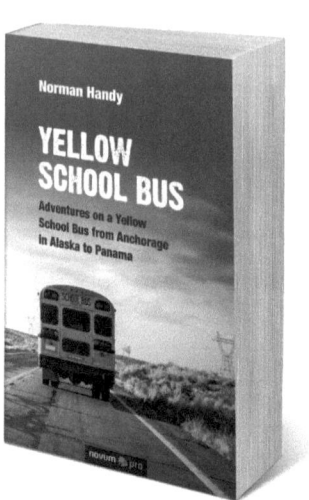

Are you an adventure buff or a travelholic? Then this one is right up your alley. Here is yet another one of Norman Handy's brilliant, exciting and interesting travelling adventures with various other travelling companions on… yes, a yellow school bus.

Norman Handy

Crossing Russia on the Trans Siberian

ISBN 978-3-99064-046-3
216 Pages

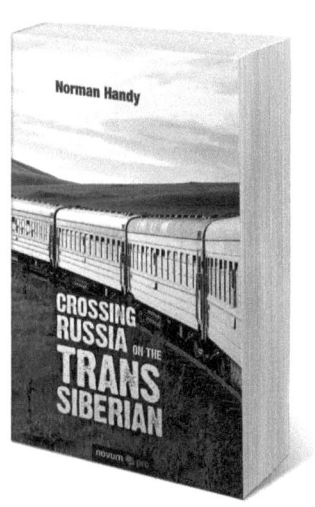

A fascinating account of a trip through Russia that will intrigue Russophiles, travellers, history buffs and adventurers alike. The author traces his journey from Saint Petersburg via riverboat and the Trans-Siberian Railway, to his destination, Vladivostok.